CATCHING
THE WAVE

When one wants to ride a wave all the way to shore, one must catch the wave at its apex, just before it begins to break, and then get on top of the wave for the ride of your life. Readers are in for just such an experience if they get on board with Tim MacBride's new book *Catching the Wave*, and stay on board all the way to the conclusion. No one I know does a better job of translating the ancient rhetoric of the New Testament for twenty-first-century listeners, showing how the ancient art of persuasion can provide us with models not only for understanding but also for preaching the New Testament. Tim has indeed caught the wave of modern rhetorical studies of the New Testament at precisely the right moment and time and provided his audience with a means of understanding and applying the New Testament in fresh ways. Highly recommended!
Ben Witherington III, Amos Professor of New Testament for Doctoral Studies, Asbury Theological Seminary; Doctoral Faculty (Emeritus), University of St Andrews, Scotland

Catching the Wave is not a work residing in the lofty atmosphere of the abstract: rather it is a concrete compendium for the immediate use of its intended readership. It will be a homiletic shower for the parched and needy academy and church. MacBride believes that sermons need to be informative and transformative. He advocates a reunion of *what the text says* (exposition) and *what the text does* (function) in an effort to prevent stylistic sermons with little informative or transformative value. I recommend *Catching the Wave* with the highest confidence.
Robert Smith Jr, Charles T. Carter Baptist Chair of Divinity, Beeson Divinity School, Samford University

CATCHING THE WAVE

Preaching the New Testament as rhetoric

TIM MacBRIDE

INTER-VARSITY PRESS
36 Causton Street, London SW1P 4ST, England
Email: ivp@ivpbooks.com
Website: www.ivpbooks.com

First published 2016

British Library Cataloguing-in-Publication Data
A catalogue record for this book is available from the British Library.

ISBN: 978–1–78359–436–8

Set in Monotype Garamond 11/13pt
Typeset in Great Britain by CRB Associates, Potterhanworth, Lincolnshire
Printed and bound in Great Britain by 4edge Limited, Essex

*Inter-Varsity Press publishes Christian books that are true to the Bible and that
communicate the gospel, develop discipleship and strengthen the church for its mission
in the world.*

*IVP originated within the Inter-Varsity Fellowship, now the Universities and Colleges
Christian Fellowship, a student movement connecting Christian Unions in universities and
colleges throughout Great Britain, and a member movement of the International Fellowship
of Evangelical Students. Website: www.uccf.org.uk. That historic association is maintained,
and all senior IVP staff and committee members subscribe to the UCCF Basis of Faith.*

CONTENTS

ACKNOWLEDGMENTS

I've been writing this book, in a way, for more than fifteen years.

In 2000, as a second-year seminary student, I was to preach on a particular passage from 2 Corinthians. After spending a few weeks with various commentaries, I felt as if I knew *what* Paul was saying in my assigned text, but I still had no idea *why* he was saying it – what he wanted his audience to do in response. This meant I still didn't know what my sermon was going to do, either. And time was running out. It was then that I stumbled across the field of rhetorical criticism – via Ben Witherington's commentary on the Corinthian letters – which focused not just on what texts *said*, but also on their function. Not only did this help with the immediate problem of my sermon the following week, but it set me on a lifelong quest to work out how understanding the function of a biblical text could, or indeed *should*, impact the function of our sermon on that text; or, to use Michael Quicke's words, how to design 'a sermon that says *and does* the same things the biblical text says *and does*'.[1]

So my first acknowledgment should be to my guides through the world of New Testament rhetoric, whose names appear in the footnotes of this book; and especially to Ben Witherington, who –

---

1. Michael J. Quicke, *360-Degree Preaching: Hearing, Speaking, and Living the Word* (Grand Rapids: Baker Academic, 2003), pp. 53, 131.

following the ideal for ancient rhetors – has taught me not only by his words, but also by his conduct, and has become a good trans-Pacific friend in the process.

The next acknowledgment is to my longsuffering congregation at Narwee Baptist Church in Sydney, Australia. In the decade following that light-bulb moment with 2 Corinthians, they were the laboratory in which I tested theories of how rhetorical analysis could inform preaching, gradually becoming aware that one day I'd write a book about it. I got to discover what worked – and what didn't – in a supportive environment. (And I apologize for the times that it didn't work; in particular, for a 2005 sermon on Philemon. Even now, I still don't think I quite know what to 'do' with Philemon.) All of the sample sermons in this book are real sermons preached to this congregation as I sought to put theory into practice. Speaking of theory, the influence of the church's senior minister and my long-time colleague, Angelo Gratsounas, can be found on most pages of this book: a naturally gifted preacher, he has little patience for theory that doesn't yield any practical benefit. I think largely because of his influence, I've sought to give examples of how each aspect of rhetorical theory presented in this book has practical pay-off.

In 2009 I decided that this quest I'd been wrestling with each week as I prepared sermons would become the topic for my doctoral research. This could not have been done without the support of Morling College in Sydney, Australia, through which I completed my studies, and at which I'm now privileged to teach each day. I couldn't ask for a more supportive (or fun) group of colleagues! The writing of this particular volume was facilitated by Morling College's generous gift of study leave.

Acknowledgment must also be made to the Australian College of Theology for, among many other things, publishing my thesis (in 2014) on which this more reader-friendly book stands.

Thanks also to Tim Chavura, for reading with 'fresh eyes' an early draft of this book and offering helpful feedback. And to Philip Duce and the team at Inter-Varsity Press, for giving me the opportunity to present these ideas to a wider audience.

Finally, thanks go to my wife and children for supporting me in this journey over the past fifteen years, and allowing me the time and space to write – even to the point of turning down the volume on *The Simpsons* whenever I happened to be writing a particularly challenging paragraph in the next room.

Tim MacBride
February 2016

INTRODUCTION: SERMONS THAT *DO*

Language doesn't just *say*. It also *does*. We all know this.

When a parent announces to a child, 'There are dirty clothes all over the floor', it isn't just a statement in the indicative: there's an implied command. The intended response isn't 'Yes, that's an accurate observation of the state of my room.' The child is supposed to pick the clothes up – to *do* something in response.

When a wife asks her husband, 'Does my butt look big in this?', she's not looking for an objective answer to her question. She's asking him to reassure her that he still finds her attractive.

Language doesn't just say. It also does.

Catching the wave

It's just as true when it comes to the language of the Bible. The biblical authors didn't just communicate *content* – they also wanted their words to *do something* in the lives of their first hearers.

When God asked Adam in the garden, 'Where are you?', it wasn't because God couldn't locate him; it was an invitation to a difficult but necessary conversation. When God answered Moses from the burning bush, saying, 'I am who I am', it wasn't an attempt to avoid the question, nor merely an acknowledgment that God can't be adequately described in words; it was also an implicit call to 'watch this space' as God would soon reveal his character by his actions.

The Gospel writers, too, didn't record certain words and deeds of Jesus out of historical curiosity, but explicitly 'that you may know the certainty of the things you have been taught' (Luke 1:4), and 'that you may believe that Jesus is the Messiah, the Son of God, and that by believing you may have life in his name' (John 20:31).

And the apostle Paul didn't just write a treatise on justification by faith and then, as an afterthought, send a copy to the Christians in Rome. He clearly wanted this letter to *do something* in the lives of the recipients. (What exactly that might have been is the subject of much scholarly discussion – and goes to the heart of what this book is about, as we'll see shortly.) Paul's epistles don't just seek to inform, but to persuade, to exhort and, ultimately, to transform.

So if the biblical text we're preaching on not only says things but also does things, doesn't it make sense for our sermons not only to say those same things but also to do something similar? A quick survey of the last thirty years of preaching writers would suggest that the answer is 'yes'. For example:

> David Buttrick: 'The question, "What is the passage trying to *do*?" may well mark the beginning of homiletical obedience.'[1]
> Fred Craddock: 'Does the sermon say and do what the text says and does?'[2]
> Thomas Long: A sermon on a given biblical text also has a focus *and function*, and both of these 'should grow directly from the exegesis of the biblical text'.[3]
> Michael Quicke: 'Scripture not only says things but also does things.' The task of preaching is 'designing a sermon that says *and does* the same things the biblical text says *and does*'.[4]

---

1. David Buttrick, 'Interpretation and Preaching', *Interpretation* 25 (1981), p. 58.
2. Fred B. Craddock, *Preaching* (Nashville: Abingdon Press, 1985), p. 28.
3. Thomas G. Long, *The Witness of Preaching*, 1st edn (Louisville: Westminster John Knox Press, 1989), pp. 189–190.
4. Michael J. Quicke, *360-Degree Preaching: Hearing, Speaking, and Living the Word* (Grand Rapids: Baker Academic, 2003), pp. 53, 131. Quicke himself is consciously building on the work of Craddock and Long.

As preachers, we spend a lot of energy trying to recover the original meaning of a text and to interpret that meaning for a new audience. Having dutifully explained the content, we then search for 'application' – another way of saying that we want our sermon to do something in the lives of our hearers. This, however, is often the point at which we leave the text behind, and through a process of prayer, cultural attentiveness and pastoral concern we make the text do something useful for our congregation.

Fair enough. Yet if the biblical texts themselves are already trying to do something, shouldn't we try to find out what that 'something' is? Given the energy that goes into recovering the original meaning, shouldn't we also spend a similar amount of energy trying to understand the original *function* of a text, so that our sermon might function in the same way for our hearers?

It's a bit like the difference between swimming against the current and catching a wave. If we take the content of our biblical passage and then try to do something with it that the original author didn't intend, we often find ourselves paddling against the force of the text. However, if we work out what the author was trying to achieve in the lives of the original audience *and attempt something similar in our own context*, we're putting ourselves in the best place to catch the wave and harness the power of the text. When the function of our sermon lines up with the original function of the Word, the power of the Spirit is more likely to wash over us and our hearers.

But how do we catch that wave?

A question of rhetoric

We'll come back to that question shortly, because forty years ago – when writers like Buttrick and Craddock were pioneering the so-called 'New Homiletic' – there was another wave forming on the horizon. It was all about studying the rhetoric – the *persuasive intent* – of a text. It got a label back in 1968 when the president of the Society for Biblical Literature, James Muilenburg, called for research in a field he termed 'rhetorical criticism'.[5] This call was answered by pioneers like Hans Dieter Betz in his commentary on Galatians; George Kennedy, applying his classical education to the study of the New Testament; and, in the two most recent decades, Ben Witherington in his prolific output of socio-rhetorical commentaries. The field is by now well worn and established.

Now, there are various types of rhetorical criticism.[6] Some apply universal theories of rhetoric to texts. Others look at how texts can be used for rhetorical purposes alien to that of the original author. The kind I'm interested in here, however, is what's usually termed the 'historical' sort – in particular, as it relates to the New Testament epistles. This discipline looks at the rhetorical rules and terminology of Graeco-Roman oratory, taken from the speech-writing handbooks of the day and other ancient sources. That is, it's based on how the ancients *themselves* theorized about persuasive speech. Having looked at this theory, it then seeks to understand the New Testament epistles in these terms, as speeches. After all, most epistles were intended to be read out loud, given the lack of universal literacy and limited access to photocopiers.

In essence, rhetorical criticism looks at the biblical text and asks not just what the text was intended to *say*, but also what it was intended to *do* in the lives of its first hearers. It sees an epistle by Paul, for example, as an exercise in rhetoric – that is, persuasive speech – following, by and large, the rhetorical conventions of his day. Rhetorical criticism provides a framework to understand the *function* of a biblical text, using the very tools first-century writers would have used to construct the text in the first place.

So far, nothing I've said is particularly new. I've just summarized what's been happening in the area of preaching theory and New

---

5. James Muilenburg, 'Form Criticism and Beyond', *Journal of Biblical Literature* 88 (1969), pp. 1–18.

6. Some people can be put off by the term 'criticism', given the negative connotations of how we use the word in ordinary speech, or its association with liberal methodologies. Its usage here, however, simply reflects a German word that is about making judgments. Call it 'rhetorical analysis' if you prefer.

Testament research. And what I want to suggest is simply this: that the question being asked by the New Homiletic can be answered, at least in part, by rhetorical criticism. All we need to do is to tie these two strands together.

In other words, how do we 'design a sermon that says and does the same things the biblical text says and does'? Answer: through rhetorical criticism, we can find out not just what the text was saying to its first hearers, but also what it was intending to *do*. From that, we can develop a systematic approach that helps us create our sermon, so that it functions in the same (or very similar) way.

My aim in this book is to take this very simple idea and show how we might be able to use it to inform the function of our sermons. First, we'll be introduced to the three different kinds – or genres – of speeches in the ancient world. This is because each genre performed a different function and was appropriate for a different setting in public life. Second, we'll look at the form of an ancient speech, since each element of the speech structure had a different function in relation to the whole. Third, we'll investigate the ways in which ancient writers attempted to persuade: *ethos*, based on the character of the speaker; *pathos*, seeking to arouse emotions in the audience; and *logos*, appealing to reason. At each point we'll stop to see examples of how this plays out when we preach from the epistles, to see what it might be like to 'catch the wave'.

Some assumptions

Before we get going, here are a few of the basic assumptions I'm working from.

Throughout the book, we'll be looking at examples drawn mainly from Paul's letters. The reason for this is that out of all the New Testament books, they appear most closely to follow Graeco-Roman speech conventions, particularly in form and genre. The exceptions are 1 and 2 Timothy and Titus, as they are more like 'mandate' letters than written-down public speeches. The other epistles (and Revelation) still exhibit this to varying degrees – especially in terms of the rhetorical strategies used. The Gospels and Acts are less relevant as they are biography/historiography rather than public speeches;

however, Paul's speeches as recorded in Acts follow the conventions of courtroom rhetoric discussed in chapter 1.

I'm also assuming that it's legitimate to view most of Paul's letters as written-down speeches. I think we can do this as long as we're cautious, and don't try to fit *everything* into the textbook models. If you're interested in a defence of why we can apply first-century *speech*-writing theory to the *letters* of Paul – including the issue of whether Paul was trained in rhetoric – see Appendix A, along with chapter 2 of my previous book.[7]

My previous book is also the reason for proceeding with the minimum of footnotes here. If you want references to the ancient sources and critical argument in all their scholarly pretension, that's where you'll find them. The aim of *this* book is to make the idea simple and accessible to those wanting to use it in preaching, rather than to defend the methodology. It's a 'how to' guide, rather than an academic argument.

Finally, I'm explicitly assuming an expository preaching model. Without dismissing the important role of the topical sermon, I believe that expository, text-based preaching should be the bread and butter of regular congregational preaching. Of course, the term 'expository' is used in various ways, and has frequently been associated with verse-by-verse explanations and a deductive approach – not to mention points that all conveniently begin with the same letter of the alphabet. However, my definition is more in line with the New Homiletic I mentioned earlier. I consider a sermon to be expository if it seeks to *say and do* what the text says and does, no matter what form the sermon eventually takes. In other words, I'm outlining an approach for *creating* a sermon rather than for a particular style of delivery.

Enough about assumptions. We've paddled out through the breakers, and now we're ready to catch a few waves.

---

7. Tim MacBride, *Preaching the New Testament as Rhetoric: The Promise of Rhetorical Criticism for Expository Preaching*, Australian College of Theology Monograph Series (Eugene: Wipf & Stock, 2014), pp. 22–34.

PART 1

GENRE

In this part we'll look at the importance of understanding the rhetorical genre (type of rhetoric) of an epistle. There were three kinds of speeches in the ancient world. We'll briefly touch on all three in the first chapter, showing how rhetorical genre determines the overall aim of the text – and our sermon.

The next two chapters focus on two of the genres which are found frequently in the New Testament, to see how we might preach from these genres. (The forensic rhetoric genre is much rarer, so it doesn't get its own chapter.) A sample sermon is given at the conclusion of chapters 2 and 3.

1. PREACHING AND RHETORICAL GENRE

Ladies and Gentlemen of the jury . . .
We are gathered here today to celebrate the life of . . .
Men and women of Australia . . .

Three kinds of speeches. Three different settings in community life. One in a law court, seeking to persuade its hearers of the truth about something that happened in the past. One at a funeral, seeking to remind those who have gathered of the praiseworthiness of a person in the present. And one in political discourse, seeking to persuade its audience of a particular decision or course of action for the future. These are, essentially, the three kinds or *genres* of speeches identified by Aristotle and his contemporaries. He termed them forensic (*dikanikos*, in Greek), epideictic (*epideiktikos*) and deliberative (*symbouleutikos*).[1] Each had a different setting in the life of the ancient world, and each had its own persuasive goal.

---

1. Aristotle, *Rhetoric*, 1.3.3. See also *Rhetoric for Herennius*, 1.2.2; Cicero, *On Invention*, 1.5; Quintilian, *Institutes of Oratory*, 3.14.16.

The three kinds of rhetoric

Forensic rhetoric arose in the courtroom. Originally, a person bringing an accusation to the court, or defending against one, was expected to speak on his or her own behalf. Over time, people began to hire speech-writers to craft their speeches for them, and eventually to have the speech-writers deliver the speeches in their place. And so the practice of attorneys and clients was born. The aim of both sides was to persuade the crowd (and thereby the judge) of the truth or falsehood of the accusation being brought. This meant it was focused on what happened *in the past*, and the argument centred on what is *just*.

Outside the courtroom, this kind of speech could be used to attack or defend – most commonly in politics, when trying to discredit opponents or defend against slander. It's relatively rare in the New Testament, although Paul's speeches before the Jews (Acts 22:1–21), Felix (24:10–21) and Agrippa (26:1–30) are clearly forensic. They're described by Luke as a 'defence', using the technical term *apologia*. Some see 2 Corinthians as being essentially forensic, where Paul defends himself against charges of being fickle (1:17) and just in it for his own gain (2:17).

By contrast, *epideictic rhetoric* belonged to festivals and public events. Its name means 'display', and it was designed to display the honour and worth of a person, a god or even a moral value. (It also came to be used in some quarters to display the skill of the speaker, which is the kind of rhetoric Paul avoids in Corinth. We'll talk about this later in the book.) Such a speech could also be called an *encomium* or a *eulogy*, and was – as it is today – employed at funerals. However, the ancients didn't wait until people were dead to speak well of them. Great war heroes or visiting dignitaries would be honoured by eulogies at festivals as a way of reinforcing already-held cultural values. The aim was to elicit praise for the subjects and inspire people to emulate them. This meant it was focused on the *present*, and the argument centred on what is *honourable*.

In the New Testament, several epistles are generally thought to be epideictic in character. In 1 Thessalonians, Paul praises the values of the Thessalonian believers in order to inspire them to even greater heights. In 1 John, the author encourages his hearers to hold fast to community values in the face of a recent departure of some separatists from the group. And in Ephesians, Paul eulogizes God, inspiring both praise and emulation.

Deliberative rhetoric was essentially a product of Greek democracy. To make decisions about future policies and actions – such as waging war, balancing the budget or increasing the supply of olive oil in the gymnasium[2] – citizens gave speeches for and against the proposal. They would try to persuade the hearers of the benefits (and justice) of their proposed course of action, and the dangers of the alternatives. The assembly would weigh the arguments and vote for whichever was the most persuasive. This meant it was focused on the *future*, and the argument centred on what was *advantageous* to the citizenry as a whole.

Most of the rhetoric in the New Testament is deliberative in character, trying to persuade the people of God to live a certain way, both because it's the right thing to do (in the light of what God has done for us) and because it's ultimately to their advantage. Many of the surviving political speeches from this era were appeals for the members of a group or city to be *united* for the sake of the common good. As we'll see later, in several of Paul's epistles the basic appeal is for unity: in Romans he argues for unity between Jews and Greeks on the basis that each has been saved the same way – through faith (1:16–17); in 1 Corinthians he appeals for unity in a faction-ridden church (1:10); and in Philippians he advises unity as the believers' 'civic duty' in the face of opposition (1:27–28).[3]

Summary: The three kinds of rhetoric

Genre	Goal	Time focus	Primary question
Forensic	Attack/defence	Past	What is just?
Epideictic	Praise/blame	Present	What is honourable?
Deliberative	Advice	Future	What is to our advantage?

---

2. This was a more important issue than you might imagine. The city might be under attack, or bankrupt, but as long as there was enough oil for men to rub on each other, everything was OK.

3. It's interesting that Paul uses this method – persuasion, rather than giving instructions – even to churches he founded. Christian leadership is not coercive.

Determining the rhetorical genre

This may be all well and good in theory, but how do we go about identifying the rhetorical genre of a biblical text?

In the early days of rhetorical criticism the tendency was to jump quickly to an opinion about genre and then try to force every part of the text into that framework – producing wildly different results from different scholars. These days there's a more mature process and the results, for the most part, are approaching enough of a consensus to aid our preaching. Here's a quick guide to the process.

First, realize that the ancient rhetorical handbooks themselves speak of mixing the types of rhetoric. There may, for an example, be an epideictic section of a speech that is, overall, deliberative in its aim. This was considered 'good form' in longer speeches, to give the audience some variety. A good example of this is 1 Corinthians, which is a long, deliberative speech, urging unity. Chapter 9 is a forensic section which defends – he even uses the technical term *apologia* in verse 3 – Paul's refusal to accept financial support from the Corinthians, a key part of his overall deliberative appeal for unity. And chapter 13 ('Love is patient, love is kind . . .') is an epideictic passage in praise of love *as a unifying force*. Understanding the role of such sections in supporting the overall argument helps in correctly identifying the overall genre.

Second, note the topics being discussed in the letter and the types of appeal being made. This was an important addition to the process made by Margaret Mitchell,[4] who studied surviving copies of actual speeches, along with the handbooks. She noticed that certain types of rhetoric were used to address certain topics; for example, deliberative rhetoric was often used to appeal for civic unity. She also pointed out that both in theory and in practice, the different types of rhetoric used different types of appeals. As we saw above, forensic rhetoric focused on justice, epideictic on honour, and deliberative on advantage. Noticing the subject matter and types of appeal being made will point us to the type of rhetoric being used.

---

4. Margaret M. Mitchell, *Paul and the Rhetoric of Reconciliation* (Louisville: Westminster John Knox Press, 1993).

This leads to a third factor, often called the 'rhetorical situation'. This is similar to what traditional commentaries label the 'occasion and purpose'. In determining the *rhetorical* situation, however, we're looking not just at the historical and social situation of the sender and receiver of the letter, but at what the text intends to *do* in that situation. Again, certain types of rhetorical situation call for certain types of speech. For example, if a community needs to choose one course of action over another, deliberative rhetoric is likely to be employed. However, if a community needs its existing values reinforced in the face of opposition, epideictic is more natural.

Finally, especially when beginning in this field, it's important to consult a variety of rhetorically aware commentaries – particularly recent ones written after the first flush of rhetorical enthusiasm! Ben Witherington's commentaries are a good place to start, as is the recent Paideia series from Baker. In Appendix B I've provided a very brief guide to the rhetorical genre of the relevant New Testament epistles, along with lists of a few recommended commentaries that take a rhetorical approach.

Summary: Determining rhetorical genre

Be aware of the possibility of mixed genres.
Note the subject matter and types of appeals used.
Reconstruct the rhetorical situation.
Consult a variety of commentaries.

Rhetorical genre and the aim of the sermon

So how does all this help us preach from one of these epistles? In the next two chapters we'll look at some implications specific to deliberative and epideictic rhetoric. First, though, some general points about rhetorical genre and preaching.

The aim of the sermon
Most importantly, understanding the rhetorical genre of an epistle tells us a lot about its purpose – what it's trying to *do*. This then

informs the purpose of our sermon if we're serious about our sermon doing what the text did. Or, to put it diagrammatically:

Rhetorical genre → Purpose of the text → Purpose of the sermon

The significance of this for preaching shouldn't be underestimated. To begin with, it reminds us that the text is trying to *do* something. Some sermons can give the impression that the biblical text was written simply to inform us about something – to give us knowledge. We leave the sermon informed, not transformed, because knowledge is only a means to an end. By looking at the text as rhetoric – persuasive speech – we're reminded of this most basic principle: the text itself has a purpose, and if we're to be faithful to the text, its purpose should also be the purpose of our sermon, broadly speaking.

Further, identifying the rhetorical genre helps us guard against the purpose of our sermon being at cross purposes with that of the text. If a text is deliberative, advising the most advantageous future course of action, we ought not to preach a sermon that is primarily forensic, defending a biblical truth. If a text is epideictic, celebrating a value already held and urging us to continue to live by it, we ought not to preach a sermon that is primarily deliberative, warning those who choose not to live by it of the future consequences. In other words, an epideictic text should be preached *epideictically*. A deliberative text should be preached *deliberatively*. (This will be the focus of the next two chapters.)

For example, a forensic text has as its primary aim to *prove* something to be true. This should also be the primary aim of the sermon. It means that there may be very limited practical application other than belief in the proposition being proven. This can be difficult in situations where the vast majority of the (believing) congregation is already in hearty agreement with the proposition. However, we can ask questions in the light of the rhetorical situation about *why* the author felt the need to prove it. This may open up links to our own situation and then suggest lines of application. It can also function as an example of how *we* might go about defending that particular truth in our own context.

For example, Paul's speech to Agrippa in Acts 26 is a forensic defence of the thesis that Jesus fulfils what the prophets spoke about

– namely, 'that the Messiah would suffer and, as the first to rise from the dead, would bring the message of light to his own people and to the Gentiles' (26:23). The immediate function is evangelistic, as Paul is trying to persuade Agrippa of this truth. This could also be its function in an explicitly evangelistic sermon. However, the speech also functions within the narrative of Acts to affirm the faith of those who already believe (cf. Luke 1:4) and as a paradigm for defending the gospel, with the implication that it can withstand rational scrutiny by educated people (cf. elsewhere in Acts: 13:7; 17:11). In other words, if we look at *why* Luke records this forensic speech it may help our sermon to connect more readily with a congregation made up primarily of believers.

Forensic texts will most naturally (though, of course, not necessarily) fit with a deductive preaching model.

An epideictic text primarily seeks to honour already-held community values (e.g. 1 Thess. 1:3–10; 3:6; 4:9) as a means of encouraging stronger adherence to them (cf. 1 Thess. 3:11; 4:1, 10; 5:11). A great injustice to the text is done if such a text is preached in a negative way, berating our hearers for their failure to live out these values. While this may sometimes be true of a given congregation, the rhetorical strategy employed by such a text is exactly the opposite! For example, a sermon series through 1 Thessalonians – if it's to respect the rhetorical genre – might look within our own community for positive examples of the gospel values mentioned in the text and hold them up as an inspiration for the whole.

Deliberative texts are perhaps the least mistreated in contemporary preaching, as they focus on more application-friendly questions of 'How should we then live?' However, we need to ensure our sermon is in fact urging a course of action compatible with the intent of the text, rather than an action of our own invention (no matter how 'biblical' it may be). Often an understanding of rhetorical form can help us in this, as we'll see in part 2. Deliberative texts are also the most suited to inductive approaches, as we lead our hearers in seeing the 'advantage' of the righteous or godly course of action in the light of the alternatives.

The kinds of appeals

Determining the rhetorical genre also helps us to be alert to the kinds of appeals being made in the text and – by now this shouldn't come as a surprise – the kinds of appeals we might make in our sermon. A deliberative sermon on a deliberative text will focus on showing how following God's way (as opposed to the world's way) is to our ultimate advantage. An epideictic sermon on an epideictic text will try to evoke praise of the subject (God, or a particular value) and inspire emulation in increasing measure. We'll talk more about this in the next two chapters.

The rhetorical situation

Finally, understanding the rhetorical genre also helps us work out the rhetorical situation – that is, the story of what's going on in the world of the writer and recipients, and what the writer is trying to *do* in that situation.

This isn't a new concept. The goal of the historical-critical method has been to reconstruct the 'setting and purpose' of an epistle. However, an understanding of rhetorical genre helps us work out that setting more closely, and focuses us on the *purpose* aspect.

You might have spotted a problem here. At the start of the chapter, we were using the rhetorical situation to help determine the rhetorical genre: if the audience needs to be persuaded to do something in the future, the genre is probably deliberative, and so on. Here, though, we're using the rhetorical genre to help determine the rhetorical situation: if the genre is deliberative, the audience must need to be persuaded to do something in the future. Isn't this getting a bit circular? How does that work?

There *is* a certain circularity to it. The indications of genre (the topic, the kinds of appeals being made, formal characteristics, etc.) help us identify the rhetorical situation, and the rhetorical situation alerts us to what genre might be employed by a speaker in that situation. It's an iterative approach, to see if the picture 'fits'. In other words, our initial impression of the genre might be that it is deliberative, and so we use that to help understand the rhetorical situation. This should then feed back into the issue of genre and either confirm it or question it. If the latter, we go back and do it again, until we get a good fit between the two.

The pay-off for accurately determining the rhetorical situation is significant. It helps us to lay the foundations of the 'preaching bridge' by asking if there are situations in our own world which are similar to what was going on in the world of the text. Having identified these similarities, we then ask what kind of transformation might be desirable among our hearers in the light of the text. That is, we begin to ask whether the text might have something very similar to *do* in our own situation.

To give a very simple example, as we prepare to preach through Galatians and try to reconstruct the original situation, we start to ask questions like this:

1. What kind of Judaizing tendencies do we see within our churches today?
2. What is the rhetorical function of Paul's argument in Galatians in seeking to transform that situation?
3. How might this argument speak into our own context as we preach it?

(The sample deliberative sermon at the end of chapter 2 gives a further example of this process, beginning to 'apply' the original rhetorical situation to our own.)

Conversely, we also note the *differences* between our own situation and that of the original audience. This helps us see how we might have to alter the rhetorical purpose of our sermon to take into account these differences. (After all, in most churches I've been to there isn't the looming threat of knife-wielding Judaizers running a circumcision rally.)

These are only preliminary thoughts at this stage, as the rest of the process outlined in this book will lead us into more concrete answers – and possibly in unexpected directions. Already, though, our understanding of the original rhetorical situation of the text should be shaping the connection between the world of Paul's hearers and our own.

Summary: Identifying rhetorical genre helps us . . .

Make the aim of the text the aim of our sermon.

Know the kinds of appeals our sermon will make.

Reconstruct the rhetorical situation and see links with our own situation.

Preaching mixed genres

There's one last issue to do with genre that we need to look at. We alluded to it before: it's when we're preaching from a section of text which has a different genre from the overall epistle. How, then, do we establish the goal of the text – and the goal of the sermon – when there are competing genres in play?

The key lies in identifying three things:

1. The goal of the smaller unit of text being preached;
2. The goal of the entire epistle;
3. How the goal of the smaller unit contributes to the overall goal of the epistle.

Let's look at two examples from 1 Corinthians to see how this works. Remember, the overall epistle is *deliberative*, urging concord and an end to factionalism. However, there are two chapters which employ a different genre.

The first is 1 Corinthians 9, which is a defence (*apologia* in 9:3) of Paul's practice of being 'all things to all people' (9:22). His *ethos* (character) is in question throughout the letter, particularly as people were comparing his rhetorical prowess unfavourably with that of Apollos. This was exacerbated by Paul's insistence on working for a living, which was considered demeaning for a travelling teacher, rather than receiving financial support from the Corinthians. He did this to avoid the appearance of patronage, in which he would have become indebted to his financial supporters and therefore part of the status games going on in the church. However, he did accept support elsewhere (e.g. Phil. 4:10–20) where the same social dynamics weren't in play. This opened Paul up to the charges of being an inferior apostle (one who had to work for a living), as well as being *changeable*. This would have been given some weight by Paul's advice in the surrounding chapters relating to food sacrificed to idols. His advice seemed to change depending on the circumstances (compare the different advice in 1 Cor. 8:4, 13; 10:21, 25, 28).

In 1 Corinthians 9 Paul defends himself against these charges, arguing that he does indeed have the right to earn a living from the gospel, but chooses not to so that he's not bound by their patronage

(9:18). Further, he points out that, while his behaviour may indeed be changeable, his *guiding principle* is always the same: he gives up his own rights for the sake of the gospel, becoming like those he's trying to reach – all things to all people.

When preaching this chapter, the forensic goal should be uppermost in mind. We defend the same principle of 'all things to all people' against any opposition that might be around today to 'sit in judgment' on us (9:3). To those in our churches who accuse us of selling out to the surrounding culture, we point out that we're simply following Paul's (and Jesus') example of becoming like those we're trying to reach. To those who complain that they want things the way *they* want them, we point to Paul's example as our defence. We are defending, here, the principle of incarnational ministry.

To leave it there, however, is to miss the wider deliberative goal of the epistle: unity and an end to factionalism. Why is Paul defending himself here, in this letter? Because he's hurt and wants to set the record straight? No – it's because their diminished view of Paul was causing *division* in the church. By defending his 'all things to all people' principle he's doing two things. First, he's addressing one of the reasons some were divided against Paul, in order to end the factionalism that had arisen. Second, he's illustrating from his own actions a key principle that leads to unity: giving up one's rights for the good of others. (He sums this up in 10:32 – 11:1.)

Our sermon, then, will seek to connect the forensic goals of the passage with the overall deliberative aims of the epistle. A defence of incarnational ministry promotes *unity* in our churches because it seeks to undercut division over ministry practice *and* it embodies the wider principle of putting others first. Or, to put it more simply, it tells us: *stop fighting about having things the way you prefer them, and focus on the preferences of the people you're trying to reach with the gospel!*

A similar situation is found in 1 Corinthians 13. Here, Paul uses *epideictic* rhetoric to praise love as a virtue, in order to encourage his hearers to love all the more. However, he only does this because it contributes to the overall aim of the letter – producing unity in the church. So a sermon on this chapter should also praise selfless love in order to encourage our hearers to love all the more – but the explicit context and purpose of this love should be to produce a

united fellowship. It's not primarily designed for use at weddings
(although it can be!) but to promote love *in the church*.

Summary: When preaching mixed genres . . .

Find the goal of the unit being preached.
Keep in mind the overall goal of the epistle.
Work out how the goal of the smaller unit contributes to
the larger goal, and make the connection in the sermon.

Over the next two chapters we'll focus on issues specific to
preaching the two rhetorical genres found frequently in the New
Testament: deliberative and epideictic.

Exercise

Read the following passages and attempt to identify the rhetorical
genre of each section of text (not necessarily that of the entire
epistle from which it is drawn), using the knowledge you have gained
thus far.

- Revelation 2:1–7
- Acts 22:1–21
- Hebrews 11

Once you've had a go, turn to the notes on the next page.

Notes on the exercise

The letters to the seven churches in Revelation 2 and 3 are *deliberative* in character. Each sets out two contrasting courses of action with contrasting consequences, urging the hearers to do what is right and to their ultimate advantage.

Acts 22 is one of a number of *forensic* speeches Paul makes to defend himself (see the word 'defence' in v. 1) against the accusations made by the Jews (see 21:28 for the specific accusation). He narrates the facts of his case in order to show that he is doing God's will – which goes reasonably well until he mentions *Gentiles* . . .

Hebrews 11 is an *epideictic* interlude in praise of faith. The eulogizing of faith – through the examples of faithful people throughout Israel's history – serves the epistle's overall deliberative aim of encouraging its audience to persevere in faith, prioritizing eternal reward over temporary security (see 12:1–3).

2. PREACHING DELIBERATIVE RHETORIC

As we saw in the previous chapter, deliberative rhetoric grew out of civic council deliberations where speakers would try to persuade the hearers to do something. Paul uses deliberative rhetoric in most of his epistles, seeking to persuade the people of God to live God's way.

The key characteristics of deliberative rhetoric are a focus on *future* behaviour, appeals to what is *advantageous* to the hearers and the use of *examples* to persuade. We'll look at each of these characteristics now, to see how it might make an impact on our preaching.

A focus on the future

First, let's state the obvious: if the overall aim of the biblical text we're preaching on is to persuade the original hearers to embrace a future course of action, then the overall aim of our sermon should likewise urge a future course of action for our hearers. It should confront people with a choice of behaviour or attitude to adopt into the future.

When the future focus is unclear

This may seem straightforward, but what about texts containing, for example, a dense theological argument? There might not be an obvious future course of action being urged *in the smaller textual unit itself.* We need to go back to the overall aim of the larger unit, as indicated by the overall genre of the epistle. We need to see how the argument contributes to this overall aim, and align our sermon application (the 'so what?') with that bigger picture.

This is a great help in finding application from a text which seems to be an abstract theological argument. For example, throughout Romans 1 – 8 a variety of theological issues is addressed, such as the sinfulness of humanity, the nature of justification and original sin, to name just a few. Our sermon may indeed *inform* our congregation of Paul's teaching on these subjects – and possibly even persuade some to conform their beliefs to the biblical teaching – but what's the call to action? Having identified Romans as deliberative rhetoric, we look at how each section of the letter contributes to Paul's overall argument about *future* behaviour. We see that each of these theological explorations provides the foundation from which Paul can persuade his audience – and from which we can persuade ours – *don't think you're better than anyone else based on race or on any other social division, because we're all saved the same way.*

Similarly, in Galatians 3 – 4 there are some detailed arguments about the relationship between faith in Christ and observance of the Mosaic law. A sermon that focuses on the fact that God's promise preceded the giving of the law (Gal. 3), or on the way Paul depicts those who still insist on obedience to the law as being children of the slave woman Hagar (Gal. 4), might be *interesting* – or not – but what should our congregation do in response to such a message? As deliberative rhetoric, the overall future appeal of Galatians is to not go back to the slavery of the law – because what we have now in Christ is far superior! Although this point isn't explicit in every section of Galatians 3 – 4 we might preach from, it's the *rationale* for it all. So the 'action point' from each sermon will be similar: in the light of this teaching, *don't add religious rules or cultural boundary markers to the gospel of faith.*

When the future focus is less relevant

A second, less-obvious issue is a hermeneutical one: Is the proposed future course of action still relevant today? Or was it specific to the original time and culture? For example, a deliberative epistle urging hearers not to turn, or return, to Judaism may be less relevant to a contemporary Gentile audience. So our sermons may instead need to urge an analogous course of action. The future focus of a sermon on, say, a section from Hebrews may be: you're not likely to want to adopt Judaism, but don't be seduced by any other cultural or religious worldview just because it might be the easier path (in the short term). Jesus is still superior to that, too.

Further, a text urging the wearing of head coverings (1 Cor. 11) or obedience to an authoritarian state (Rom. 13) will require even more interpretive work. For example, what was Paul trying to *do* in the original rhetorical situation by urging the wearing of head coverings? Are there analogous situations today where we could achieve a similar end through a *different* action? In other words, is there a transcultural principle in Paul's rhetorical strategy, even if the specific action he urges is no longer appropriate?

This isn't an issue unique to rhetorical criticism, of course – it's basic hermeneutics. However, rhetorical theory can help focus our thinking by asking of a deliberative text: what future behaviour is it urging, and (most importantly), *why?*

Appeals to advantage

Another key characteristic of deliberative rhetoric is how it seeks to persuade. It tries to demonstrate the *advantage* of the proposed course of action over against the *disadvantage* of the others.

A long-running TV advertising campaign in Australia has been for superannuation funds that are run as an industry cooperative, rather than for profit. The cornerstone of the campaign has been to contrast the future retirement wealth of a person who invests in an industry fund with that of someone who uses one of the for-profit funds. The clear message is: look at the long-term advantage of an industry fund, and make the right decision. This, in essence, is a deliberative appeal to advantage.

Now, cynically, we could see this strategy as appealing to a selfish, 'what's in it for me?' attitude, but two factors count against this. First, in the more collectivist, first-century Mediterranean culture, the advantage tends to be for the whole community ('the common good') rather than for individuals. 'What's best for all of us?' might be a better way of phrasing it. Second, in the New Testament it's often promoting ultimate advantage over against temporal advantage: that is, you might suffer hardship, shame or loss in *this* life, but remaining loyal to Jesus pays off in the age to come.

Appeals to advantage in the New Testament
Here's a very quick tour of some of the places where Paul appeals to advantage, just to give an idea of the 'flavour' of it.

For a start, he frequently uses the technical terminology of such arguments – such as *beneficial, benefit, the common good, reward, better, gain, not in vain* – although our English translations often don't make this clear.

Paul regularly contrasts that which is advantageous with that which is disadvantageous: in Philippians 3:7–11 he considers his works of the law to be like rubbish that he might *gain* Christ. Later on in that chapter (3:19–21) he contrasts the fate of the Judaizers who chase temporary advantage with the eternal reward for those who hold fast to Christ:

> Their destiny is destruction, their god is their stomach, and their glory is in their shame. Their mind is set on earthly things. But our citizenship is in heaven. And we eagerly await a Saviour from there, the Lord Jesus Christ, who, by the power that enables him to bring everything under his control, will transform our lowly bodies so that they will be like his glorious body. (Phil. 3:19–21)

Paul also argues that something is *even more* advantageous than something else that is beneficial: in 1 Corinthians 7 he says that while marriage is good, it's *better* for a person not to marry so that he or she might be more fully devoted to Christ. In Philippians 1 he acknowledges that it is *better by far* for him to depart to be with Christ, yet it's for the Philippians' advantage that he remain.

Indeed, the advantage of the group is often at the forefront of Paul's thinking. In 1 Corinthians 6:12 he notes that, while everything might be permissible, not everything is *beneficial*. The context shows that he's thinking of what is beneficial for the common good, not just for the individual. More generally, several of his letters deal with the topic of 'concord' (1 Corinthians, Philippians and probably Romans). It was a truism that concord, or unity, was to the advantage of the whole community, while discord, or factionalism, was to its disadvantage.

There's plenty more, but I think we get the idea. (An interesting exercise would be to go through all of Paul's deliberative epistles and highlight the appeals to advantage. You'd end up with a colourful Bible!) Note also that Hebrews is one big, long appeal to the advantage of Christ over Judaism, and 1 Peter argues for the advantage of belonging to God over fitting in with the pagan world.

Preaching appeals to advantage

So what does this mean for our preaching?

First, we must identify any appeals to advantage in the text and apply them to our own hearers. We should ask whether they are still appropriate; if not, how else might we appeal to advantage? For example, in Philippians 3, although the disadvantage of relying on Jewish works of the law might be less relevant, what other religious and cultural boundary markers might be similarly to our disadvantage in the light of the supreme advantage of gaining Christ? In Hebrews, although the attraction of Judaism as a tolerated monotheistic religion in a pagan empire no longer exists, what other religions and worldviews function similarly today? Often the advantage of remaining true to Christ hasn't changed in two thousand years, but the disadvantage of the alternatives may differ in the detail.

Second, the idea of 'group advantage' (the Greek word is *sympheron*) needs to be rehabilitated in the current me-focused era. Our world increasingly caters for individual preferences in just about anything (the second person pronoun in YouTube is most definitely singular) and emphasizes personal satisfaction as the supreme good. When we preach 'advantage' texts we need to make sure we're not simply reinforcing this idolatry, serving up what people's itching ears want to hear (through earbuds on their own individual iPods, at a time and place of their choosing). New Testament appeals to advantage are frequently plural and focus on the common good of the believing community as well as the good of each individual within it.[1] Our preaching must likewise match this corporate focus.

Third, if the text appeals to advantage, our sermon should do likewise – rather than appealing to guilt, which is often the default. Sure, if the text commands, then command; but if the biblical author is using a strategy of persuasion, trying to show that following God's pattern for life is to our advantage, shouldn't our sermon do likewise?

Henry Cloud says that sermons often use guilt as a motivator which, as a psychologist, he says is doomed to failure as a means of effecting change. By contrast, Cloud encourages people to 'play the movie forward'. He gets people to map out in detail how their lives will play out if they continue in their current patterns of behaviour, and then to contrast that with what will happen if they change. In essence, Cloud is advocating the use of appeals to *advantage* as a key motivator in creating change.[2] Where the New Testament uses this strategy for its original hearers, it makes sense both hermeneutically and pragmatically for us to use it with our own audiences.

In fact, deliberative rhetoric in general encourages an inductive preaching model. This is where we guide a congregation through different attitudes and behaviours, evaluating each in terms of its relative advantage, until we lead our hearers to the conclusion that what Scripture is urging is indeed the wisest and most beneficial course of action.

Use of examples

Our final key characteristic of deliberative rhetoric is the use of examples to persuade. Instead of merely using deductive proofs from logic, it uses an inductive approach. Drawing arguments from

---

1. See especially 1 Cor. 12, with its use of *sympheron* in v. 7.
2. Henry Cloud, *9 Things You Simply Must Do to Succeed in Love and Life* (Nashville: Integrity, 2004), pp. 69–94.

the world around us (analogies) and from other people, past and present (examples), it builds up a pattern that illustrates the benefit of following the advice given. However, other kinds of rhetoric use this strategy too, so we'll leave this one until chapter 11 to deal with it more fully.

Summary: When preaching deliberative texts . . .

Determine the future focus.
- Sometimes we will need to go back to the overall aim of the larger unit to find it.
- Sometimes we will need to look at the underlying principle.

Bring out the appeals to advantage in the text.
- If they are no longer as relevant, recast them for our own culture.

Emphasize the 'common good' rather than individual advantage.

Persuade the audience of the benefits rather than using guilt.

Exercise

1. Identify the deliberative strategies used in Revelation 14:6–13.

- What is the future focus?
- What are the appeals to advantage and disadvantage?
- How would you preach this passage?

2. Read Hebrews 10:19–39.

- What is the future course of action being urged?
- What are the appeals to advantage and disadvantage?
- What examples does the writer use to build his case?

This second passage from Hebrews is the text for the example deliberative sermon which follows.

A DELIBERATIVE SERMON

This sermon on Hebrews 10:19–39 was preached in January 2013 and draws on the strategies outlined in chapter 2. I've left it written 'for the ear' to keep it as close as possible to what was actually said. Comments on the strategies used are made in the boxes.

Introduction

Following Jesus isn't easy. Jesus didn't say it would be. And it isn't.

The temptations to give up are all around us – the pressures to conform to how the rest of the world lives – particularly, I think, at this time of year. During my holiday break, I kept a bit of a mental diary of the pressures I saw:

> Begin with a basic sermon introduction raising the difficulties we face today as followers of Jesus.

For starters, there's the culture of leisure. At this time of year, everyone's taking it easy – why not let that spill over into your spiritual life? Let that slide a bit. Replace it with televised sport. It seems minor, but it then makes us more vulnerable to all the other influences around us.

One day, while going to the beach, I walked past a luxury villa. It looked a bit like the evil lair of a 1970s-era Bond-villain (probably why it appealed to me). But it makes you think: would life be easier by now if I'd done what everyone else does and chased material success rather than God? (Probably not: shark pools are a nightmare to clean. And planning for world domination really eats into your leisure time. But still, it plays on your mind.)

Then, the other night, one of my kids complained about the bombardment of interest-free shopping ads on TV at the moment, pounding us with the message: you must have it *now*. Why wait? Despite the fact we've just been given a whole lot of stuff for Christmas. We're relentlessly reminded that we exist to spend, to consume, to enjoy. In the middle of that, following Jesus – the one who said 'Deny yourself, take up your cross, and follow me' – isn't easy.

Another day, I was sitting in the crowd at a Twenty20 cricket match. I overheard a group of teenagers who'd heard some fragment of the Old Testament – out of context – about a woman being the property of a man. As a result, they were mocking the entire Bible as being hilariously out of date and irrelevant. I almost said something in defence, but I knew I had only a few seconds before stadium music started up again – and also that any effective argument would probably take at least half an hour of explaining the nature of Scripture in its historical context. (If I'd been at a Test match, maybe I'd have had a shot.) But it left me with the feeling that, a lot of the time, defending the faith is too hard.

And then, a couple of days later, I was talking about the gospel with a Muslim friend. Now she had a great openness to talking about religion – but only within a framework where there were no exclusive claims to truth. We could talk about Jesus, about Mohammed, about the gospel – as long as, at the end of the day, everyone was right; as long as there wasn't *one* right answer. Which seems to be the way most conversations with most people go these days when it comes to talking about faith. Talk about Jesus if you have to, *just don't try to convert me.*

They're just a few things that happened to me during my holidays. Small things. I'm sure you could add a few examples of your own. But they're part of a bigger picture: a society that slowly pressures us away from following Jesus, or at least into not taking him too seriously; that tries to replace him with wealth and pleasure; and then marginalizes his claim to speak for the one true God using ridicule or ignorance.

Following Jesus isn't easy.

Background to Hebrews

And yet, that isn't a new observation. You might have noticed that in our Bible reading today. Although it was written almost two thousand years ago, the letter to the Hebrews was addressed to a similar world: to a minority group facing pressure to conform to the rest of society.

In fact, they were a minority group *within* a minority group. They were most probably Jews – already a minority treated with suspicion by the rest of society. And *Christian* Jews at that – those who'd abandoned the faith of their family and broken with their community – to follow Jesus.

> Now draw the parallels (and note the differences) between the original rhetorical situation and our own. Doing this early in the message shows our audience how the text might speak to us.

And this had been costly. As we heard in the Bible reading, in the recent past they'd suffered much. Public insults and persecution. Attempts by their family, by the Jewish community, to shame them back into conformity. Some had their property taken away from them. Others were even thrown into prison for their faith. And everyone in the church had suffered the day-to-day pressure of being different from their family; being different from the society around them; living by different values; working for different goals.

To the point where, for some, it had become too hard. They'd started to long for their former life: a life where they had been accepted by their community, when they were like everyone else. Sound a bit familiar?

And so they'd begun, little by little, to draw back from being identified with Jesus. Giving up meeting together with their fellow believers. Living again as Jews under the old covenant. Forgetting the fact that the sacrifice of Jesus had rendered it obsolete. Subtly at first, some were tempted to give it all away. The price of following Jesus was too great. They just wanted to be normal again.

So this letter to the Hebrews (really, it's a written-down sermon) was given to counteract the pressure to conform.

It's a bit like a half-time locker-room speech by a coach, urging his team to keep going, reminding us of three great truths that will help us persevere. And although they're

> Explicitly describe the rhetorical strategy used, showing how it's still appropriate for us today.

found *throughout* the letter to the Hebrews, we see them all very clearly just in today's reading. Let's have a look at them now.

We persevere – because of what we have in Jesus (10:19–25)

The first reason we persevere is because of what we have in Jesus – or, to put it more bluntly, because of the *advantage* we gain from following Jesus.

> Introduce and explain the first argument from advantage.

This was one of the big motivators used by speakers in the first century: to persuade people to do something because it was to their *advantage*, their gain.

And the writer to the Hebrews is no exception. In fact, the overarching theme of his sermon is this very idea: that following Jesus brings far more *advantage* than sticking with Judaism; that fearlessly identifying ourselves with Christ brings far more *gain* than fitting in with whatever *our* society tells us to do.

And he gives a kind of recap of his arguments so far: the summation of all those complicated arguments about Jesus being greater than angels, greater than Moses, greater than the Levitical priests; that his sacrifice is greater than those of the Old Testament. The recap begins at verse 19. So let's take a look at the *advantage* we have in following Jesus.

> Therefore, brothers and sisters, since we have confidence to enter the Most Holy Place by the blood of Jesus . . . (10:19)

What's the Most Holy Place? Well, for the Jews it was the inner shrine of the temple, where the ark of the covenant was kept, where God symbolically 'lived' among them. It was cut off from the rest of the temple by a thick curtain, just like the first-class seating on a plane. And no-one was allowed in – except for once a year, on the Day of Atonement, when the high priest could go in, but only after an elaborate ritual of purification and sacrifice. It symbolized the fact that God is holy and we're not. We're not fit to be in the presence of the almighty God. That's the truth which lies at the heart of the Jewish sacrificial system.

So why would anyone want to go back to *that*? I mean, when Jesus has made it possible for us to enter not just an earthly sanctuary but the heavenly one? We have direct access to God himself! Not just once a year, but whenever we like. And how did this happen?

> since we have confidence to enter the Most Holy Place *by the blood of Jesus, by a new and living way opened for us* through the curtain, that is, his body . . . (10:19b–20)[3]

It happened through Jesus' sacrifice of himself for us: his death in our place. He opened up a new way for us with his own blood. He put his body on the line for us. In fact, there may be a military background to this expression; the idea of 'opening up a new way'.

In Greek history, the story is told of a heroic military commander Decius Mus, about three hundred years before Christ. The battle was getting nowhere. So he decided instead to lead from the front. The historian Florus records that he went out 'hurling himself where the enemy's weapons were thickest, [so that] he might open up a new path to victory along the track of his own lifeblood'.[4] Like a blocker in American football, he went through clearing a path for his army to follow: a new way through his blood.

That's what Jesus did for us. He opened up a new way, at the cost of his life.

A trailblazer. Or a 'pioneer', as the writer to the Hebrews puts it in chapter 12. Jesus has cut through the defence. He's made the hard yards. All we have to do is run through the gap.

> Recast the first-century metaphor (battle) into a contemporary one (sport) – see chapter 11.

But it's not just what he's done in the past; he's *still* on our side in the present.

> and since we have a great priest over the house of God . . . (10:21)

We have Jesus *acting on our behalf* right now. Interceding for us with the Father. Our advocate. Our defence attorney. Which gives us confidence; gives us assurance:

---

3. All emphasis in Scripture quotes is mine.
4. Florus, *The Epitome of Roman History*, 1.9.

> let us draw near to God with a sincere heart and with the full
> assurance that faith brings, having our hearts sprinkled to *cleanse*
> *us from a guilty conscience* and having our bodies *washed* with pure water.
> (10:22)

We're no longer unclean before God. We no longer have to shrink back from his presence because of our sin. We've been cleansed of guilt, because of Jesus' sacrifice in our place. We've been washed clean in his sight, by Jesus' lifeblood given for us.

> Let us hold unswervingly to the hope we profess, *for he who promised is*
> *faithful.* (10:23)

Added to all this is the very character of God himself: 'he who promised is faithful': is trustworthy; is reliable.

Why, then, given all this *advantage*, would you want to go back to your old ways? The old sacrificial system? The old barriers that kept God at a distance? Why would you shrink back from following Jesus, when there's so much to *gain*?

You wouldn't, would you? That's how the writer wants us to respond. Instead of being held back by fear of public opinion, he urges us to 'draw near' to God; to hold *unswervingly* to the hope we have in Jesus; to publicly identify ourselves as his followers, no matter what the cost. As an act of trust, that God will look after us if we do.

Don't be drawn back into the life everyone around us is living. Because there's no advantage, *no gain.* And now, we have everything already in Christ! Why would we *want* to fit in with a society that's alienated from God, guilty and without forgiveness, and with no hope for the future? Instead, be *proud* that you're different. Be unashamed of being identified with Jesus.

And part of that, the writer continues, is being identified with Jesus' followers: meeting together with fellow Christians.

> And let us consider how we may spur one another on towards love and
> good deeds, not giving up meeting together, as some are in the habit of
> doing, but encouraging one another – and all the more as you see the
> Day approaching. (10:24–25)

We meet *together* as believers for the primary purpose of encouraging one another to live God's way, not the world's way. It's insulation against the lure of the world.

We 'spur one another on towards love and good deeds'. The word 'spur' here can be translated as 'provoke' or even 'irritate'. So, as Christians, we can *irritate* one another?! Well, I'm sure you can all testify to that. But the idea here is that we urge one another to keep living God's way. We prick one another's conscience. And sometimes that *might* be irritating – but it's for our good.

One of the keys to perseverance, one of the ways in which we're reminded of how good we've got it with Jesus, is meeting together. We remind ourselves of what Jesus has done for us, and how anything else that the world might throw at us is *inconsequential* in the light of what we now have.

Please don't give up meeting together – both here at church and in your small groups. Because I think this is a *particular* danger for this present generation, for two reasons.

First, if you went back only thirty years ago – back to when I was a kid – you'd find a very different attitude to church attendance. If you were a serious Christian, it'd be two services on a Sunday – unless you were away, sick or dead. Church attendance was an outward measure of your spirituality.

These days, we see that as legalistic. God looks at the heart, not at how many services you turn up to. Big tick for us. Except I think we've now swung too far the other way. In exercising our freedom from being under law, we've allowed other things to crowd it out. For many – not just here, but across the Western world – church has become something we fit in when we can. A movie session time we pick and choose from, if there's nothing better on. An option, rather than a commitment. Our retreat from legalism has to some extent become lawlessness.

This is made more acute by a *second* factor: the increasing pace of life. Our society demands more and more from us, just to keep up with it. In most parts of our city, two incomes are now a necessity. So households have less time to get things done around the home. Getting to work takes longer. There's more and more stuff to do. So as well as being *less committed* to meeting together, we tend to have *less time* as well.

I've seen it happen with my own friends. They slowly drift away from God, they shrink back into the world – initially because they didn't make time to be with God's people.

Yet the Bible tells us to make church community a priority.

> Apply the rhetorical appeal to advantage to our own situation.

Not so we can count big attendances and pat ourselves on the back; but because it's a vital part of how God intended us to persevere. Not to shrink back, but to stay the course.

We draw near to God by drawing near to his people. Because it's only when we're *with* his people that we'll be constantly reminded of all that we have in Christ. And how much greater that is than what the world has to offer.

We persevere – because of what we have in Jesus.

We persevere – because the alternative is unthinkable (10:26–31)

> Explain the difficult text in the light of the rhetorical situation and strategy.

The second strategy the writer uses is a more negative one.

We persevere, he says, because the alternative is unthinkable. To shrink back from following Jesus, to return to the world – it's both dishonourable and to our disadvantage. Have a listen to how he puts it:

If we deliberately keep on sinning after we have received the knowledge of the truth, no sacrifice for sins is left, but only a fearful expectation of judgment and of raging fire that will consume the enemies of God. (10:26–27)

The previous context is important here. This *isn't* a general statement about sins a believer might struggle with. If it were, I don't think there'd be a person listening who wouldn't be in trouble. But in context, this is about those who know the truth of God and the deliverance he provides – but who still choose the temporary benefits of friendship with the world. They count the cost of following Jesus and decide it's too great; that the benefits Jesus brings are not worth the suffering. In doing so, they've cut themselves off from the only means of being free from sin. And they're left without any further way of salvation.

Have a listen to how this attitude is described:

> Anyone who rejected the law of Moses died without mercy on the testimony of two or three witnesses. How much more severely do you think someone deserves to be punished who has trampled the Son of God underfoot, who has treated as an unholy thing the blood of the covenant that sanctified them, and who has insulted the Spirit of grace? (10:28–29)

That is, what such people are doing is dishonourable. They've trampled the Son of God underfoot, they've insulted the Spirit of grace, they've shown contempt for God's offer of salvation. They've looked at God's favour and thrown it back in his face, because they preferred the rewards and respect of the world.

A writer by the name of David deSilva puts it this way. It's very challenging, but listen to what he says:

> If we care more about success, respect or being wise as this world defines it, if we keep following its rules and set our ambitions on its promises, we trample upon Jesus. We set too little value on his blood if we refuse to walk in that life for which he freed us. We insult God's favour if we seek to secure the world's favour first and then, as far as the world will let us, God's promised benefits.
>
> If your first thought is for keeping our neighbours' or coworkers' or fellow citizens' approval, and if we seek to live out our Christian life within the parameters of the kinds of behaviours or words that will not 'offend' the unbelievers, we show by our lives whose approval really matters to us, and we insult God.
>
> A special danger faces the Christian in the modern, secularized world . . . Our tendency is to attend dutifully to everything else our society tells us is important and then to give religious concerns any leftover time, resources and energy. Again, such an approach to life

says to God, 'your gifts and call are not of the first order of importance in my life'.[5]

| Now contrast it with the alternative – and point out the ultimate disadvantage. |

But not only do we *dishonour* God in this way.

In the end, it's to our *disadvantage*. The writer to the Hebrews ends this section with a stern warning:

For we know him who said, 'It is mine to avenge; I will repay,' and again, 'The Lord will judge his people.' It is a dreadful thing to fall into the hands of the living God. (10:30–31)

No matter how badly the world will treat us: that's *nothing* compared with what awaits those who remain unforgiven; those who *reject* God's grace. If you jump out of the frying pan of persecution, you only end up in the eternal fire.

We persevere – because the alternative is unthinkable.

We persevere – because that's who we are (10:32–39)

Heavy stuff. That's the negative motivation. But you'll notice that it's sandwiched in between two bits of positive motivation. The first point was that we persevere because of what we have in Jesus.

| Explain the appeal to example. |

And the final point is: we persevere because that's who we are. That's what we do.

And to kick this point home, the writer appeals to a whole range of examples of those who remained faithful despite hardship.

Their Israelite ancestors. The forerunners of the faith. In chapter 11, he drags out the Old Testament hall of fame. Or, rather, hall of faith.

---

5. David A. deSilva, *Perseverance in Gratitude: A Socio-Rhetorical Commentary on the Epistle 'to the Hebrews'* (Grand Rapids: Eerdmans, 2000), p. 373.

But he begins this series of examples with perhaps the most persuasive example of all. Their own.

> Remember those earlier days after you had received the light, when you endured in a great conflict full of suffering. Sometimes you were publicly exposed to insult and persecution; at other times you stood side by side with those who were so treated. You suffered along with those in prison and joyfully accepted the confiscation of your property, because you knew that you yourselves had better and lasting possessions. (10:32–34)

Not so long ago, he says, you proved yourselves faithful. You endured everything that got thrown at you. And did so *with joy*. Why? Because you knew that what you have in Jesus is *far greater* than anything the world offers. *Far greater* than anything you've lost.

So all you have to do is live up to your own reputation. Your own example. Remember what you've already resisted – because if you don't, your previous courage will be forgotten. The sacrifices will have been for nothing. Don't waste it all by throwing it away now:

> So do not throw away your confidence; it will be richly rewarded. You need to persevere so that when you have done the will of God, you will receive what he has promised. (10:35–36)

As the fourth-century preacher John Chrysostom comments on this passage: 'Powerful is the exhortation from deeds [already done]: for he who begins a work ought to go forward and add to it . . . And he who encourages, does thus especially encourage them from their own example.'[6]

In fact, there's an example of this from about the time Hebrews was written. The historian Tacitus quotes a famous general motivating his troops in this way. The general said: 'I would quote the examples of other armies to encourage you. [But] As things are, you need only recall your own battle-honours . . .'[7]

---

6. Chrysostom, *Homilies*, 21.1.
7. Tacitus, *Agricola*, 34.

Remember your past deeds. Don't let them go to waste. Keep going. Live up to your reputation.

And it's what God would say to us, too.

> Apply the same strategy to our own situation.

You've come this far. Don't let it be for nothing. Because some in our own church have given up a lot for the sake of the gospel. Some have been rejected by parents because they've followed Jesus. I know someone whose parents didn't go to their wedding because they were marrying a Christian. Someone whose parents tried to hide their car keys every Sunday afternoon so they couldn't go to church. Someone who got treated as an outsider by their family for deserting the Orthodox faith. And the list could go on.

Others have faced rejection at work. Loss of promotion opportunities. Loss of friendship and community at work. Loss of respect of their peers.

Many others have faced financial loss because they've heard the call of God to work full-time for the kingdom; maybe to go overseas to share the gospel; or maybe to give *sacrificially* so that others might go.

As it is with every church throughout the world, we've given up some of the comforts and respect of this world for the sake of the gospel.

Don't let that go to waste now.

> Bring home the comparison of advantage/disadvantage.

Don't shrink back, just because it might be seeming that little bit harder at the moment. Remember what you have in Jesus, meeting together regularly to gain strength. Remember the alternative – and how terrifying that is. And live up to your reputation.

The writer concludes the chapter a bit like a primary-school teacher before an excursion, or somewhere the kids have to be on display, on their best behaviour. You know the technique: after warning the class in a stern voice about the fearsome punishment that awaits those who misbehave, the tone suddenly changes. 'But *we're* not going to be like that, *are* we, Year Two?' And the kids all go: 'Noooo . . .' Give them a reputation to live up to, and then show you're confident they can do it.

Not much has changed in two thousand years:

> For, 'In just a little while, he who is coming will come and will not delay.'
> And 'But my righteous one will live by faith. And I take no pleasure in
> the one who shrinks back.' *But we do not belong to those who shrink back* and
> are destroyed, but to those who have faith and are saved. (10:37–39)

Live up to who you are. It's not much longer, and Jesus will return.
So keep going.

Put up with the fact that the unrighteous seem to prosper –
for now.

Put up with the fact that you might be giving up wealth and success *in this life*. There *is* another one to come.

> Show how this has spoken to the issues raised in the introduction.

Put up with the ridicule you get for following an ancient book that isn't always straightforward to interpret. Put up with the patronizing attitude you encounter whenever you're bold enough to suggest that maybe there *are* right and wrong answers to the great questions of life.

> Therefore, since we are surrounded by such a great cloud of witnesses,
> let us throw off everything that hinders and the sin that so easily
> entangles. And let us run with perseverance the race marked out for us,
> fixing our eyes on Jesus, the pioneer and perfecter of faith. For the joy
> that was set before him he endured the cross, scorning its shame, and
> sat down at the right hand of the throne of God. Consider him who
> endured such opposition from sinners, so that you will not grow weary
> and lose heart. (12:1–3)

We persevere – because of what we have in Jesus.
We persevere – because the alternative is unthinkable.
We persevere – because that's who we are.

3. PREACHING EPIDEICTIC RHETORIC

In chapter 1, we learned that epideictic rhetoric had its home at festivals and public events. It displayed the honour and worth of its subject, which could be a person, a god or even a moral value in the abstract. Its aim was to *praise* the subject and to hold the subject up as an example for *emulation*, as a way of re-inforcing society's values. (It could also be used to shame those who didn't live by society's values, holding the subject up as a negative example to be avoided.) Epideictic rhetoric was focused on the *present*, and the argument centred on what was *honourable*.

Epideictic techniques in the New Testament

Before we look at how we might go about preaching from epideictic texts in the New Testament, we need to get a sense of its 'flavour'. If we look at the speech-writing handbooks from the period, we see lots of space dedicated to outlining the many categories under which someone might be praised, and the techniques that could be used to do so.[1] Here's a very quick tour as it relates to the New Testament.

Categories for praise

We could spend a long time listing all the categories and sub-categories mentioned in the handbooks, but they mostly boiled down to the four cardinal virtues: wisdom (often called prudence), self-control (temperance), courage (fortitude) and justice. To these you could add other virtues like generosity, splendour and gentleness, as well as noble birth (genealogy) and physical prowess, but you get the basic idea. The aim in writing an epideictic speech was to work through the various categories to show how praiseworthy your subject was in each of those ways. You'd do this by recounting the subject's virtuous actions and achievements, which were evidence of a virtuous character. And you'd single out for special mention actions that were done for the sake of others – often at significant personal cost – or that were rare or unique.

Even just a quick look at the first chapter of Ephesians shows how the New Testament authors could apply these categories to the praise of God. For example:

- Splendour: 'to the praise of his glorious grace' (1:6);
- Generosity: 'grace, which he has freely given us . . . that he lavished on us' (1:6, 8);
- Wisdom: 'that he lavished on us. With all wisdom and understanding . . .' (1:8);
- Strength: 'his incomparably great power for us who believe. That power is the same as the mighty strength he exerted when he raised Christ from the dead' (1:19–20).

Later on in Ephesians, Paul directs praise to Christ for bringing peace (2:14–16), a great benefit for which the Roman emperor was traditionally praised. And he especially highlights the self-sacrificial

---

1. If you're interested, look at Aristotle, *Rhetoric*, 1.9; Quintilian, *Institutes of Oratory*, 3.7; and the anonymous *Rhetoric for Herennius*, 1.6.

nature of Christ's actions, using a phrase commonly used to praise benefactors[2] who put themselves at risk for the sake of others:

> live a life of love, just as Christ loved us and *gave himself up for us* as a fragrant offering and sacrifice to God . . . Husbands, love your wives, just as Christ loved the church and *gave himself up for her.* (Eph. 5:2, 25)

Paul also praises the Thessalonian believers using similar categories in his first (epideictic) letter to them. And wherever there's a doxology in the New Testament, you'll see these categories pop up:

- Romans 11:33: 'Oh, the depth of the riches of the *wisdom* and *knowledge* of God!'
- Ephesians 3:20: 'Now to him who is able to do immeasurably more than all we ask or imagine, according to his *power* that is at work within us . . .'
- Jude 25: 'to the only God our Saviour be *glory, majesty, power* and *authority* . . .'

Techniques of amplification

So, once you'd drawn up your list of things you were going to praise your subject for – thanks to the handy categories found in the handbooks – how would you go about it? The handbooks had that covered, too.

The main way you'd do it was through a technique called *amplification*, which was about making your subject look bigger and better. Actually, it was really a collection of techniques. Here's a very quick rundown,[3] again using Ephesians as our source of examples.

- *Augmentation*: using strong words, painting the actions of the subject in the best possible terms, and using superlatives:

---

2. Frederick W. Danker, *Benefactor: Epigraphic Study of a Graeco-Roman and New Testament Semantic Field* (St Louis: Clayton, 1982), pp. 321–323.

3. For the longer version, see Quintilian, *Institutes of Oratory*, 8.4.

> glorious grace . . . freely given . . . lavished . . . (1:6–8)

> And God placed *all things* under his feet and appointed him to be
> head over *everything* for the church, which is his body, the fullness
> of him who fills *everything* in *every* way. (1:22–23)

> He who descended is the very one who ascended *higher than all*
> *the heavens*, in order to fill the *whole universe*. (4:10)

- *Accumulation*: piling up words or sentences that are basically
  identical in meaning, to make the argument seem all the more
  overwhelming:

> And I pray that you, being rooted and established in love, may
> have power, together with all the Lord's holy people, to grasp
> how wide and long and high and deep is the love of Christ . . .
> (3:17–18)

- *Rational argument*: giving logical reasons why the subject is
  superior:

> But because of his great love for us, God, who is rich in mercy,
> made us alive with Christ even when we were dead in transgressions
> – it is by grace you have been saved. (2:4–5)

- *Comparison*: comparing your subject favourably with another.
  You could compare subjects with their opposites, to bring
  out the contrast, or with the poorest examples in the same
  category; but most effective was comparing them with things
  that were already impressive, and showing them to be even
  greater:

> far above all rule and authority, power and dominion, and every
> name that is invoked, not only in the present age but also in the
> one to come. (1:21)

> Now to him who is able to do immeasurably more than all we ask
> or imagine . . . (3:20)

The purpose of epideictic rhetoric

So how does that help us with our preaching?

Not a lot directly, at this stage – but stay with me, because it does help us identify which texts are epideictic and what they're trying to *do*: which, as we said before, was primarily to elicit praise for the subject. So if, for example, we identify Ephesians 1 as epideictic rhetoric, the purpose of the text – and our sermon – is *not* primarily to explain the intricacies of election. It's to encourage us to praise God that he's chosen us.

However, epideictic rhetoric wasn't just about praise for its own sake: this kind of rhetoric was also supposed to inspire the hearers to do likewise. The aim was to reinforce the values already held by society, and to shame into conformity those who didn't hold them.[4] This is different from deliberative rhetoric. Deliberative sought to change behaviour; epideictic sought to reinforce commitment to existing behaviour.

In 1 Thessalonians, Paul honours the community values of the Thessalonian believers as a way of encouraging them to practise them all the more:

> As for other matters, brothers and sisters, we instructed you how to live in order to please God, *as in fact you are living*. Now we ask you and urge you in the Lord Jesus to *do this more and more*. (1 Thess. 4:1)

> And in fact, *you do love* all of God's family throughout Macedonia. Yet we urge you, brothers and sisters, to *do so more and more*. (4:10)

> Therefore encourage one another and build each other up, just as in fact *you are doing*. (5:11)

John, in his first epistle, honours the community values of loving one another, walking in the light and holding to correct belief about who Jesus is. He shames those false teachers who have caused

---

4. See e.g. Plato, *Republic*, 492b–c; Cicero, *On Oratory*, 2.9.35; Quintilian, *Institutes of Oratory*, 3.4.14.

division and recently left the community, and whose behaviour is the exact opposite: they were unloving, they were in the dark and deluded (claiming to be sinless) and they didn't believe Jesus had come in the flesh. They never truly belonged to the community in the first place. John's readers are the faithful ones, who aren't going to let this distract them from being who they were called to be!

In Ephesians, the focus moves from praise (in the first half of the epistle) to emulation (in the second half). Paul begins chapter 4 by urging, in the light of the first three chapters, a life that is worthy of God's example:

> As a prisoner for the Lord, *then*, I urge you to *live a life worthy* of the calling you have received. (4:1)

> put on the new self, created *to be like God* in true righteousness and holiness. (4:24)

God's forgiveness (praised so eloquently in the first three chapters) is to be emulated in how we forgive one another:

> Be kind and compassionate to one another, forgiving each other, *just as* in Christ God forgave you. (4:32)

There are further appeals to God's example, the height of which is the sacrifice of Jesus:

> *Follow God's example*, therefore, as dearly loved children and *live a life of* love, *just as Christ* loved us and gave himself up for us as a fragrant offering and sacrifice to God. (5:1–2)

('Live a life of' is more literally 'walk in the way of': it's the language of discipleship and emulation.)

We're to emulate God's holiness ('be holy as I am holy'):

> But among you there must not be even a hint of sexual immorality, or of any kind of impurity, or of greed, because these are improper *for God's holy people*. (5:3)

And, of course, to emulate Christ's love for the church:

Husbands, love your wives, *just as* Christ loved the church and gave
himself up for her . . . (5:25)

This is vital for preaching, as it gives us an important principle
for applying epideictic texts: *praise is implicitly a call for emulation, even
where it's not explicit in the text.*

So, for example, *all* of Ephesians provides us with an example
to be emulated – not just the more practical teaching found
in chapters 4 to 6. We apply the 'praise' texts about God not as
abstract doctrine, and not *just* to inspire praise: they should also
invite – even *demand* – imitation. (The sample epideictic sermon at
the end of this chapter, from Ephesians 2, shows how this might
play out.)

Preaching epideictic texts as celebration

In essence, we should preach epideictic texts as a celebration – of
God, and of who he's called his people to be. *How?*

First, as we've just been saying, understand the aim of the text:
to praise something and to inspire emulation. Ask: Who or what is
being praised? And how might we be called to emulate this in our
own context?

Second, be aware of the techniques used by the New Testament
authors (see above). Attempt to communicate their effect to your
own congregation. If the grandeur of God is being praised, our
sermon should make people aware of his grandeur and so praise
him. If these days this takes a PowerPoint show of distant galaxies
and a golf ball, so be it.[5] Don't be afraid to use repetition, a more
varied vocabulary and lots of comparative examples.

Third, if community values are being praised and reinforced (such
as in 1 Thessalonians, 1 John and 1 Corinthians 13), preach in a way

---

5. With apologies to Louie Giglio, *How Great Is Our God*, Passion Talk
   Series (2009; DVD; Six Step Records, 2012).

that matches the text. Celebrate what your community *is* doing, rather than berate them for *not* doing it.

James W. Thompson calls this 'preaching as remembering', following Paul's example in 1 Thessalonians and elsewhere (e.g. Rom. 6:17; 15:15). He says: 'The appeal to the memory will connect the community with its foundational story, reaffirm the liturgical expression by which the community responds to God, and *recall the community's moral norms*' (italics mine).[6]

Although this might seem an obvious conclusion, many sermons on epideictic texts begin with the assumption that their hearers are *not* displaying the value being discussed in the text. They then proceed with a tone of chastisement rather than celebration. In other words, they run counter to Paul's rhetorical strategy right from the beginning.

Instead, look for ways to celebrate how your congregation is already living out this or that value – even if sometimes you might have to search long and hard! Find examples from *within the audience*, just as the New Testament writers did. Willow Creek Church is a good example of this, regularly telling the stories of their 'volunteers' in such a way as to encourage the entire community to do likewise. Their annual 'Volunteer Sunday' includes a parade of people who serve in an unpaid capacity – along with an epideictic sermon – as a way of giving thanks to God for these ministries and normalizing volunteering as a core community value of the church.[7]

When I concluded my decade of pastoral ministry, as my final series I chose to preach through 1 Thessalonians. (I was keen to 'road test' epideictic preaching!) Our preaching team intentionally used it as a time of thanksgiving and celebration, reminding our church of who we were and what we were about as we moved into a new phase of ministry. Each Sunday, we featured the story of someone from our congregation who was in some small way living out the value in the biblical text. We found that people were reminded

---

6. James W. Thompson, *Preaching Like Paul: Homiletical Wisdom for Today*, 1st edn (Louisville: Westminster John Knox Press, 2001), p. 141.

7. Bill Hybels, *Courageous Leadership* (Grand Rapids: Zondervan, 2002), pp. 91–92.

by this to thank God for how he'd been at work in our church in some of the everyday, less-noticeable ways – and, of course, to emulate those stories in their own lives.

Preaching epideictic texts is a powerful way of reinforcing community identity and 'normalizing' the church's vision.

Summary: When preaching epideictic texts . . .

Notice the techniques being used by the author.
- What are the categories of the virtues that are being praised?
- How is the author amplifying the subject?

Harness the epideictic function of the text.

The application is praise, which leads to emulation.

Recreate the effect of the text in a way that's appropriate to your audience.

Find examples in your own congregation to celebrate and to inspire imitation.

Exercise

1. Read 1 Thessalonians 1:1–10 and identify amplification techniques.

2. Read Ephesians 2:11–22. How does it inspire praise? How does it inspire emulation? (Keep your answers in mind as you read the sample sermon that follows.)

AN EPIDEICTIC SERMON

This sermon on Ephesians 2:11–22 was first preached in 2011 and draws on the strategies outlined in chapter 3. Again, I've left it written 'for the ear'. Some of the situation-specific illustration and application has been omitted.

Eulogies

As a pastor, I went to plenty of funerals. So I've heard a lot of eulogies. All different kinds of eulogies about all different kinds of people. But did you know that all those people had one thing in common? They were dead.

Today, we're looking at a eulogy with a difference. It's a eulogy for God – who, contrary to media reports and the odd German philosopher, is certainly not dead. So why give him a eulogy?

Glad you asked!

You see, in the ancient world, eulogies weren't just for dead people. 'Eulogy' comes from a Greek word simply meaning 'a good word' about someone or something. Sure, the ancients did this at funerals, just like we do. But they'd also give these kinds of speeches while people were still alive: at public festivals, or when someone important visited the city. And they'd praise, they'd eulogize, all sorts of things: community values, valiant war heroes . . . even politicians as a way of sucking up! And, of course, they'd also eulogize their gods.

> Educate the audience about genre, which will help when they read other parts of Ephesians, too.

Paul's letter to the Ephesians – well, really, it's a *speech* to the Ephesians that he couldn't give in person. So he wrote it down and sent it with someone else to be read out loud. Paul's letter to the Ephesians is *this kind* of speech: a eulogy; a speech in praise of someone. And this is important, as it tells us about its primary purpose.

You see, this *isn't* a speech trying to prove something or defend against something – like Paul's speeches in Acts or his defence in

2 Corinthians. And this *isn't* a speech trying to persuade the audience of a particular course of action, like most of Paul's *other* letters. It's a eulogy: a speech in praise; a speech in praise *of God*.

> The function of the text is the function of the sermon.

So as we read this – or indeed, any part of Ephesians – we need to keep this in mind.

What it should be *doing* is inspiring us primarily to praise God; giving us motivation for gratitude. So as we look at this passage in chapter 2 today, that's the first question I want us to ask: How do these twelve verses inspire us to praise God? Let's take a look.

Once we were excluded

> Therefore, remember that formerly you who are Gentiles by birth . . . (2:11)

Paul was a Jew: one of God's chosen people under the old covenant. But he's speaking mainly to non-Jews in Ephesus. Why is this significant? Let's read on:

> Therefore, remember that formerly you who are Gentiles by birth and called 'uncircumcised' by those who call themselves 'the circumcision' (which is done in the body by human hands) . . . (2:11)

The Jews were circumcised, as a sign that they were God's special people. A sign that dates back to God's covenant with Abraham. A sign that says 'we belong to God'. But people from other nations, referred to as Gentiles – they *weren't* circumcised. Which means that they *didn't* belong to God.

And what's more, it meant that they were treated as second-class by those who *did* belong. This isn't just about the state of your man-bits, it's about labels. Did you notice how Paul puts it? You are *called* 'uncircumcised' by those who *call themselves* 'the circumcision'. It's about labels and status and who's in and who's out. Do you belong to God and his people? Or don't you? Paul says:

remember that at that time you were *separate* from Christ, *excluded* from citizenship in Israel and *foreigners* to the covenants of the promise, *without hope* and *without God* in the world. (2:12)

This was the state of the nations, before Jesus. They were separated from God by sin. They were excluded from being a part of God's people, because they weren't in a covenant relationship with God – which meant they had no hope.

And that was the case with us, too, before we heard the gospel and responded. This describes *our* existence. Separated from God by sin, excluded from being part of his people. Without hope, without God, and on our way to eternity without him!

This is pretty depressing, for a eulogy about someone who's not dead, isn't it? What's Paul doing?

He's setting up a contrast. A reminder of what we've been saved *from*. Because, if Paul had gone straight from verses 8–10 ('by grace you have been saved, through faith') – straight to all the benefits of knowing Jesus that start from verse 13, we'd miss the impact. We'd miss the whole point. We'd miss how *amazing* grace truly is.

And I think that's especially important for people like me – and maybe like many of you – who grew up in a Christian home, responded to the gospel at a young age. Who never really got to experience what it was like to be *without hope* and *without God* in the world. We need to grasp more fully the hopeless, horrific situation that we never really had to experience, if we're going to have anything *like* the gratitude we ought to have.

Now we are included: we have peace with God

Remember what you were saved from. Because now – now it's *so* different:

But now in Christ Jesus you who once were far away have been brought near by the blood of Christ. (2:13)

What has happened? We who were far away from God have been brought near to him; into a relationship with him. *How* did it happen?

Through the blood of Christ. Jesus' death in our place, paying the
penalty for our sin. So that we can be
friends with God again. So that we
can have *peace* with God.

> Apply the function of the
> text, showing how this isn't
> abstract theology, but a
> motivation to praise.

That's our first reason to praise;
to be grateful.

We were God's enemies, and
through no work on our part we're
now his friends. Not by works, so that no-one can boast. Praise God!

Now we are included: we have peace with one another

But we don't just have peace with *God*; we also have peace with one
another:

> For he himself is our peace, who has made the two groups one and has
> destroyed the barrier, the dividing wall of hostility . . . (2:14)

He's made peace between Jews and non-Jews, by tearing down
the 'dividing wall of hostility'. What's that? It's the law:

> [he] has destroyed the barrier, the dividing wall of hostility, by setting
> aside in his flesh the law with its commands and regulations. (2:14b–15a)

We're not talking here about God's moral law. We're talking about
the rules and regulations that set Jews apart from non-Jews. The
sacrificial system. The purity requirements. The sometimes bizarre
laws in Leviticus, banning bacon sandwiches and polycotton shirts[8]
(among many other things).

God did away with the things that divide people, that exclude:
the labels 'circumcised' and 'uncircumcised'; the existence of one
group of people who were 'in' and another who were 'out'.

All that served its purpose for a time: to have one group of special
people who were separate; who displayed to the world what it was

---

8. Lev. 11:7; 19:19.

like to live the way God intended; who in some sense *revealed who God was* to the world.

But now, in the coming of Christ, we have a far superior revelation: God himself in human flesh. Praise God! And so there's no need for that separation any longer. It's like what happened with the Berlin Wall: God tore down the artificial barrier and reunited humanity once more:

> His purpose was to create in himself *one new humanity* out of the two, thus making peace, and in one body to reconcile both of them to God through the cross, by which he put to death their hostility. (2:15b–16)

Again, it's nothing we've done.

It's not by works that we can have peace with one another. It's not through humanity getting together and settling our differences just by trying really hard. It's not through any one of the dozens of 'roadmaps to peace' in the Middle East produced by countless well-meaning world leaders. It's not through a bunch of hippies staging a sit-in and singing 'let's give peace a chance'. Nor is it by sending in a whole load of soldiers to enforce peace with guns and high-tech weaponry. Just like the supposed 'peace' the Roman Empire had created back in Paul's day.

> Translate the rhetorical function for your own audience: just as the peace Christ brings is superior to the frequently eulogized *Pax Romana*, so, too, it's superior to any other 'peace' that comes from human effort.

No. It's peace brought about by *God's* actions, not our own. Peace that came through the cross of Christ. Peace reconciling us all *to God* as the basis, the precondition, for our being reconciled to one another.

That's the basis on which we can unite: the fact that all of us, no matter what our background, no matter what our status, our race, our gender – all of us are now children of God through the cross of Christ and the indwelling of his Spirit:

> He came and preached peace to you who were far away and peace to those who were near [the out-crowd as well as the in-crowd]. For through him we both have access to the Father by one Spirit. (2:17–18)

And that's what brings us together. It makes us not strangers or foreigners, but fellow citizens – family, even!

> Consequently, you are *no longer foreigners and strangers*, but *fellow citizens* with God's people and also *members* of his household, built on the foundation of the apostles and prophets, with Christ Jesus himself as the chief cornerstone. (2:19–20)

The lynchpin holding it together is not human effort – which is just as well, given our track record. It's Christ:

> *In him* the whole building is joined together and rises to become a holy temple in the Lord. And *in him* you too are being built together to become a dwelling in which God lives by his Spirit. (2:21–22)

Praise God. For he did what we were completely *unable* to do. He brought us back from estrangement from one another in this life and estrangement from God in the next. He reconciled us to himself and reconciled us to one another. At the cost of his Son, Jesus. Praise God. What a eulogy!

> Again, apply the function of the text.

Emulation

As I said at the start, I've heard many eulogies. One time, my wife and I were at a funeral and heard a particularly glowing eulogy, painting a portrait of a wonderful, God-honouring person. My wife turned to me and whispered: 'Wow, it makes you wish you were like them.' To which I said: 'What, dead?' Apparently that wasn't the right response, and could be part of the reason I'm a lecturer now, not a pastor.

But she has a point, hasn't she? If you hear a great eulogy; or just a really nice speech at a birthday or a wedding; or even if you read a great biography or see a movie that's a true story about someone particularly inspiring – when we hear stories that eulogize someone, they often make us want to emulate them in some way.

In fact, that was one of the functions of this kind of speech in the ancient world.

By holding up those who were praiseworthy – whether gods, human beings or even abstract values; by praising that which was virtuous, it encouraged everyone to do likewise.

> Explain the secondary function of epideictic rhetoric: emulation.

To be like that hero. To live in tune with that value. To emulate the gods!

Isn't this what Paul also does in Ephesians? In praising God, are we not inspired to be more like him? In praising his Son, Jesus, are we not reminding ourselves of who it is we're supposed to be imitating?

Paul makes it quite explicit later in chapter 4:

I *urge you* to live a life worthy of the calling you have received. (4:1)

Make *every effort* to keep the unity of the Spirit through the bond of peace. (4:3)

That is, if God's a peacemaker, doesn't that inspire us to be peace-makers too, just like him?

If God was sacrificial in giving his Son for those who were alienated from him, doesn't that encourage us to be sacrificial in seeking to reconcile with those alienated from us?

If God's about doing away with man-made distinctions of race and class and gender inequity – don't you want to be about that too?

So what might that look like? What would our lives look like if we were so utterly blown away by this amazing God who makes peace, who tears down any and every source of division and exclusion, and at great cost to himself unites humanity in Christ – if we were so caught up in praise that we wanted to be like him? What would our lives look like?

> Apply the function of the text. Here, there is great freedom to choose appropriate specifics; I chose the divisions caused by race and social status.

I think we'd be more circumspect in uncritically adopting the values of the world when it comes to things like race – no matter what part of the political spectrum they come from.

We wouldn't just take on board the suspicion and outrage fuelled by the right-wing shock jocks of this world – chatting to someone from a different ethnic background over coffee at church, but then ranting along with talkback radio during the week about how *they* are destroying *our* country; wanting them to go back where they came from; and complaining about how they can't speak our language.

At the *other* end of the political spectrum, we wouldn't jump on board with naïve viewpoints that think it can all be solved by a group hug and a bit more understanding – fuelled by a worldview that sees religion as evil, and says we can make peace on our own if we all try hard enough. That doesn't acknowledge the fundamental role of sin in dividing humanity. That doesn't acknowledge the need for God. Because we can save ourselves!

Instead, we'd welcome our multi-ethnic society for different reasons.

We'd acknowledge the difficulties when different cultures mix. We'd realize the need for sacrifice on our part; that it's costly. But we'd do it because it gives us the chance to imitate our God – who didn't expect *us* to make the first move.

> This isn't just generic application about race relations, but flows directly from the text.

Because it gives us the chance to 'preach peace to those who are far away' *without even having to go very far at all!* Thousands of people who are now in this country, many of whom would have had almost no chance of hearing the gospel message in their home country, *are now living all around our church*. They could be united with us, not because they learn our language or adopt our culture, but because they reconcile with our God – the one true God of *all* peoples – so that through Jesus 'we *both* have access to the Father by one Spirit'.

Sure, it can make us uncomfortable sometimes. It can be confronting – sometimes even scary. But I don't think the cross was a walk in the park either.

And it's not just race. I think we'd see it in our attitude to social class, too. Although we like to think we're a classless society, we still divide along socio-economic lines. Often the markers are the level of education we achieved. The kind of work we do. Or whether we *have* a job or not.

If we're wanting to emulate God in removing the dividing walls of hostility, the gospel will go from us across *those* boundaries as well. We won't stay safely within our own 'kind'. We won't just adopt the prejudices of our own group, and look down on those on the other side of the line.

And we won't look upon those with less than we have and think that they somehow deserve it; that they've brought it on themselves. After all, if God had taken that attitude to us, where would *we* be?

For God so loved the world that he looked at us and said: well, if you didn't spend all your paycheque on cigarettes and alcohol, maybe you wouldn't need to pray for your daily bread. I'm not going to forgive any trespasses until you've cleaned up your act a bit and shown that you deserve to be helped. And as for sending my only Son: I've sent prophet after prophet, and where's that got me? What a waste of taxpayers' money – I mean, what a waste of grace!

> Again, the application flows from the text (v. 12, 'at that time you were . . . without hope and without God').

We were incapable of rescuing ourselves from the mess we were in – why should we expect others to be any different?

If we're to emulate our God and preach peace to those who are not only near but also far, then we will also cross those dividing walls of hostility. Not as a bunch of social-working do-gooders in our own strength, but as ambassadors of the Peacemaker himself.

His purpose was to create in himself one new humanity out of the two, thus making peace, and in one body to reconcile both of them to God through the cross, by which he put to death their hostility. (2:15b–16)

That was *his purpose.* Doesn't that make you want to praise him for it? And, in response, don't you want to make that *your purpose*, too?

PART 2

FORM

In this second part of the book, we focus on rhetorical form. Ancient speeches were made up of certain components, in a relatively predictable order. Each component had a different function:[1]

The *exordium* raised the topic being addressed and established rapport with the audience.

The *narratio* stated the facts in a legal case (forensic rhetoric), or outlined the circumstances that led the speaker to address the topic (deliberative and epideictic).

The *propositio* was the central thesis the speaker was attempting to prove or the course of action the speaker was urging.

---

1. We're using the Latin terms here, not to be pretentious but because they are used in most of the scholarly writings about ancient speeches, as well as in biblical commentaries. There are also Greek equivalents that appear in the writings of e.g. Aristotle, but they are less frequently used. Also, be aware that some ancient handbook writers give a slightly different list, as they combine *narratio* and *propositio*, or *probatio* and *refutatio*.

The *probatio* formed the bulk of the speech – a series of arguments trying to prove or support the *propositio*.

The *refutatio* sought to anticipate objections or counter-arguments, and refute them.

The *peroratio* summarized the speech and made a final, emotional appeal.

This, like any textbook formula, was a guide, not a straitjacket. Some elements could appear in a different order (e.g. the *narratio* appears after the *propositio* in 1 Corinthians), and some might be missing altogether (e.g. there was often not a *narratio* in an epideictic speech).[2] (We're going to be a bit cautious with this. Early rhetorical critics got a little carried away and tried to apply the handbook structure too rigidly to the New Testament epistles – particularly in terms of the ordering of the elements. These days, the focus is more on *function* rather than form: that is, we look for the part of the epistle that *functions* as, say, a *narratio* or a *refutatio*, rather than expecting it to appear precisely at a certain point in the speech.)

You might be thinking: so what? How does identifying the part of an ancient speech we're preaching on help us? Well, that's what the next two chapters are about. The key word, though, is *function*. If we know what part of the speech it is, we know what its function is supposed to be within the speech. And if we know the function of the text we're preaching on, we're one step closer to working out the purpose of our sermon!

Or, to put it in diagram form:

Part of speech → Function of the text → Purpose of the sermon

Over the next five chapters, we'll look at preaching from each of these parts of the speech (apart from the *probatio*, which is dealt with in part 3). This will include an example sermon from Philippians 1 and two workshops: one on the *propositio* of Galatians as a window on the rest of the epistle, and the other on 1 Corinthians 15 as an example of *refutatio*.

---

2. Margaret M. Mitchell, *Paul and the Rhetoric of Reconciliation* (Louisville: Westminster John Knox Press, 1993), p. 10, n. 33.

4. EXORDIUM

One of my favourite stand-up comedians is the UK performer Michael McIntyre. He always begins his comedy shows in exactly the same way. As the crowd cheers him onstage he shouts, 'Welcome to my Comedy Roadshow . . . right here in my favourite city of them all . . .', at which point he inserts the name of whichever city he happens to be performing in that night. Of course, everyone knows that it's completely insincere, but he's playing to the stereotype of many performers before him going back to the vaudeville days. He builds rapport with the audience paradoxically by mocking the formulaic false sincerity of the genre. The formula is, however, based on a universal truth: if you want an audience to listen to you, you need to build rapport with them right at the start. They need to like you.

Ancient speeches were no different. They began with an *exordium*, which the handbooks[1] said had three functions:

---

1. See Aristotle, *Rhetoric*, 3.14.16; Quintilian, *Institutes of Oratory*, 4.1.5; Cicero, *On Invention*, 1.15.

1. To inform the audience of the subject of the speech;
2. To capture and hold their attention;
3. To win their goodwill.

These are integrally connected, to the point where you could express it as a single function: *to capture and hold attention by foreshadowing the subject and winning the hearers' goodwill.*

The subject of the speech was foreshadowed often by providing a 'preview of coming attractions', as Witherington puts it.[2] Goodwill was established by the speaker reminding the audience of his good character and honourable intentions, as well as by praising the audience. In Paul's letters, all of this frequently came together in the opening thanksgiving,[3] in which he'd tell his audience that he prayed for them often and that he thanked God for certain qualities he saw in them, all the while giving hints of what the letter was going to be about. For example:

> I thank my God every time I remember you. In all my prayers for all of
> you, I always pray with joy because of your partnership in the gospel from
> the first day until now, being confident of this, that he who began a good
> work in you will carry it on to completion until the day of Christ Jesus.
>
> It is right for me to feel this way about all of you, since I have you in
> my heart and, whether I am in chains or defending and confirming the
> gospel, all of you share in God's grace with me. God can testify how I
> long for all of you with the affection of Christ Jesus.
>
> And this is my prayer: that your love may abound more and more in
> knowledge and depth of insight, so that you may be able to discern what
> is best and may be pure and blameless for the day of Christ, filled with
> the fruit of righteousness that comes through Jesus Christ – to the glory
> and praise of God. (Phil. 1:3–11)

---

2. Ben Witherington III, *New Testament Rhetoric: An Introductory Guide to the Art of Persuasion in and of the New Testament* (Eugene: Cascade, 2009), p. 20.
3. Letter-writing theory of the time didn't include anything like the extended thanksgivings we find in Paul's epistles; however, these thanksgivings regularly perform the key functions of an *exordium* in a speech.

Clearly, Paul's thanksgiving is designed to remind the Philippians of the rapport they have with him: how highly he thinks of them, and how he wants nothing but the best for them. However, it also foreshadows much of what the rest of the letter is going to be about: rejoicing, fellowship, the gospel and its defence, love for one another and so on.[4] In this way, it functions as a typical *exordium*.

Preaching from an *exordium*

So how might we preach from an *exordium*? (We're going to leave the question of establishing goodwill and rapport with the audience for chapter 9, when we'll look at the whole question of *ethos* as a means of persuasion in ancient speeches. Here, we'll focus on the function of gaining attention by foreshadowing what the speech is to be about.)

The first question we must ask is this: If the function of an *exordium* is simply to build rapport and foreshadow the topic of the speech – and if we are indeed serious about the function of the text being the function of our sermon – is it advisable to preach on an *exordium* by itself?

Plenty of people have done so, but in my experience such sermons become topical word studies rather than being truly expository (as I've defined it here). Paul's opening thanksgivings use phrases that are theologically rich and which provide great launch pads for topical explorations of each word or theological concept: but to do so will often be at the expense of the rhetorical intent of the text. (The exceptions might be the *exordia* of Ephesians and 1 Thessalonians, since they are epideictic texts and their function is to introduce reasons to praise.) If we do decide to preach on an *exordium* by itself, I think it should be with explicit reference to the rest of the epistle, rather than in isolation.

---

4. Ben Witherington III, *Paul's Letter to the Philippians: A Socio-Rhetorical Commentary* (Grand Rapids: Eerdmans, 2011), p. 53. See also Robert C. Swift, 'The Theme and Structure of Philippians', *Bibliotheca Sacra* 141, no. 563 (1984), pp. 234–254.

To put this more positively, we can harness this 'preview of coming attractions' feature of an *exordium* by using it to introduce a sermon series – particularly if we use all or part of the *narratio* alongside it. This is because the *narratio* (see next chapter) provides much of the information about the rhetorical situation of the epistle, while the *exordium* previews the content of what Paul wants to say into that situation. We could deliver an effective opening sermon in a series by looking at the situation described in the *narratio* and showing how it relates to our audience's situation. We could then preview how the coming series is going to speak into that situation by using the *exordium*.

Even without the *narratio* to guide us, it's important to remember the link between the *exordium* and the rest of the speech. It encourages us to ask *why* Paul is thanking God for the things that he does. When we view it not as a formulaic or generic thanksgiving before the real content of the letter starts, but as an integral part of the epistle, we start to see how it might speak into the lives of our own hearers. Given the theological richness of many such passages, we might ask:

1. How does each theological truth referred to in the *exordium* prepare the audience for the main message found in the rest of the speech?
2. How might our own audience benefit from understanding this same truth in a way that prepares them to receive that message?

For example, the *exordium* of 1 Peter contains a reference to the doctrine of election:

> To God's elect, exiles, scattered . . . who have been chosen according to the foreknowledge of God the Father, through the sanctifying work of the Spirit, to be obedient to Jesus Christ and sprinkled with his blood. (1 Pet. 1:1–2)

Although this text could be used as a classic springboard into what would essentially be a topical sermon on election (as well as sanctification and atonement), understanding its function as an *exordium* causes us to ask *why* Peter refers to these theological ideas. It foreshadows chapter 2, in which Peter gives this marginalized group ('foreigners and exiles' in 2:11) a new identity as the *chosen* and priestly people of God (2:9), implicitly as an antidote to the rejection they are currently suffering at the hands of the wider society (2:4). So rather than being an abstract discussion of the doctrine of election, our sermon will focus on our 'chosen-ness' as a source of identity in a world that relegates us, too, to the margins.

A case study: 1 Corinthians 1:1–9

A good example of this is Paul's *exordium* in 1 Corinthians. Here, the problem is social division arising from worldly values (see the *narratio* in 1:11–17). The surrounding culture's obsession with status through public oratory has found its way into the church, dividing it. Paul's central *propositio* is that they be united, not divided (1:10). However, even before we get to that, in the *exordium* notice how he's already hinting at the theological basis for the Corinthians' unity:

> To the church of God in Corinth, to those sanctified in Christ Jesus and called to be his holy people, together with all those everywhere who call on the name of our Lord Jesus Christ – their Lord and ours: Grace and peace to you from God our Father and the Lord Jesus Christ.
>
> I always thank my God for you because of his grace given you in Christ Jesus. For in him you have been enriched in every way – with all kinds of speech and with all knowledge – God thus confirming our testimony about Christ among you. Therefore you do not lack any spiritual gift as you eagerly wait for our Lord Jesus Christ to be revealed. He will also keep you firm to the end, so that you will be blameless on the day of our Lord Jesus Christ. God is faithful, who has called you into fellowship with his Son, Jesus Christ our Lord. (1:2–9)

Paul's using a rhetorical device called *insinuatio*, approaching the topic in a roundabout way, slowly dropping hints: *you know how you're all indebted to God (v. 4), and you all call upon the same Lord (v. 2), which means you all have the same status; and you know how you all have had the same spiritual enlightenment (v. 5), and how God called you into fellowship with one another (v. 9) . . . ?*

At this point, the Corinthians would be starting to get the hint, thinking: *um, so where are you going with this, Paul . . . ?*

Then Paul hits them with his *propositio* in verse 10: *so stop arguing and get along! In the light of the gospel, how can you not be united!*

> I appeal to you, brothers and sisters, in the name of our Lord Jesus Christ, that all of you agree with one another in what you say and that there be no divisions among you, but that you be perfectly united in mind and thought. (1:10)

The qualities over which they are divided – and for which they are competing in human terms – are the very things they *already* have in Christ, which is why division is so foolish!

This *exordium* also functions as a 'preview of coming attractions', with many of the key words relating to later sections of the epistle:

- 'with all kinds of speech and with all knowledge' (1:5) – mentioned in 1:18 – 4:21;
- 'blameless' conduct (1:8) – see 5:1 – 11:33;
- 'spiritual gift' (1:7) – chapters 12–14;
- the believer's future hope (1:7b–8) – chapter 15.[5]

So how might we preach from this *exordium*? At least three possible strategies come to mind, each of which in some way respects its function as an *exordium*.

First, we could follow Paul's own strategy and work steadily through his list of theological truths – grace, richness in Christ, spiritual gifts, future hope and call to fellowship – before using his 'ambush' technique at the end. We 'surprise' our audience with a similar call to unity in the light of what we have just heard.

It could work well, and at first glance is the strategy most in line with the original rhetorical function of the text. However, we also need to realize that the rhetorical situation is *not* identical. It may

---

5. Ben Witherington III, *Conflict and Community in Corinth: A Socio-Rhetorical Commentary on 1 and 2 Corinthians* (Grand Rapids: Eerdmans, 1995), pp. 88–89.

well be quite different. Our congregation may *not* be divided; and if they are, issues concerning sophistic rhetoric and charismatic gifts may not be the cause. Although Paul's message is still appropriate to present-day audiences, his strategy assumes both a specific situation *and* that his audience is aware of that situation. In other words, the 'insinuation' strategy might not be as appropriate if our audience aren't going to get the hints!

A second possible approach (which is what I chose to do) is to expose the function of the text to our hearers. That is, we start by outlining the original rhetorical situation to do with division (with the help of the *narratio*, 1:11–17). We draw points of contact with the way in which our own congregation might be similarly tempted to divide around issues of status and so on. We then show, with hindsight, how Paul's *exordium* speaks into this situation. We help our audience walk a mile in the shoes of the Corinthians, which will help them get the hints Paul drops once we go back through the *exordium*.

A third possibility is to use the function of *exordium* as a 'preview of coming attractions' to introduce the series. Having outlined the situation, we use the *exordium* to give a whistle-stop tour of each of the major themes in the epistle. This prepares our congregation for future sermons and shows the way in which each topic connects with the issue of division – both in the Corinthian church and in our own.

Mark Dever thinks this kind of 'overview sermon' is incredibly useful, seeking to make 'the point of a whole book the point of a sermon'. He bases this on the conviction that 'aspects of God and his plans can be seen most clearly not only when studying the micro-scopic structure of one phrase in one verse but when examining a book as a whole'.[6]

To this I'd add that the function of one part of a biblical text can often be seen most clearly when we examine the function of the text as a whole. Using the *exordium* as a 'gateway' to a rhetorical overview is one way of achieving this. Of course, this relies heavily on having a continuity of hearers from one week to the next, so may be more appropriate in some preaching contexts than in others.

---

6. Mark Dever, *The Message of the New Testament: Promises Kept* (Wheaton: Crossway, 2005), p. 16.

Summary: The *exordium*

Part of its function was to build rapport and establish goodwill:
see chapter 9, which is all about preaching ethos.

It doesn't stand alone, but provides a preview of the rest of the speech:

- Consider preaching it alongside the *narratio*.
- Preach it in the light of its function in the rest of the epistle.
- Think about using it as a gateway to an overview sermon of the whole epistle.

Exercise

Read the *exordium* of 1 Thessalonians (1:2–3). How does this short introduction preview the coming attractions in the rest of the epistle?

5. *NARRATIO*

'There I was, driving along, minding my own business, when suddenly, out of nowhere, this lunatic pulled out of a side street and ran straight into the side of my car . . .'

A retelling of the facts of the matter, perhaps, but certainly not in an unbiased way. The emphasis on the blameless behaviour of the speaker, the unforeseeable nature of the other person's actions and the pejorative term 'lunatic' put a particular spin on the facts – preparing whoever's listening for the point about to be made, namely, 'I'm not at fault!'

This was the function of the *narratio* in an ancient courtroom speech, and it still has its equivalent in trials today. It is a recounting of the facts in a way that puts your case in the best possible light. Quintilian called it a 'persuasive exposition'.[1] In politics or advertising, we'd call it 'spin'.

For example, in Acts 7, Stephen gives a very long *narratio* – appropriate for a forensic defence – in which he rehearses the entire

---

1. Quintilian, *Institutes of Oratory*, 4.2.21.

history of Israel. However, in the selection of material and in his
editorial comments (e.g. 7:25, 'Moses thought that his own people
would realise that God was using him to rescue them, but they did
not') his potted history is really laying the groundwork for his
counter-accusation against the Jewish leaders: *you have a history of
resisting the Holy Spirit and persecuting every prophet God has sent, and now
you've done it again by killing Jesus!*

In deliberative rhetoric, in the *narratio* you would present past
events or the present situation in a way that prepared the audience
for what you were advising them to do. It wasn't always needed if
the reason for speaking was obvious. However, since the New
Testament epistles are essentially a speech delivered by proxy, by
their very nature they usually need to narrate the rhetorical context
so the audience know the reason for the speech-letter.

For example, in Romans the *narratio* gives Paul's reason for writing
– a forthcoming visit for the purpose of mutual encouragement
(1:11–12). It also gives a brief defence against any accusation that,
if he wants to go around calling himself the 'apostle to the Gentiles',
he ought to have made it to Rome sooner (1:13–15). In 1 Corinthians,
the *narratio* shows that Paul is responding, at least in the first instance,
to reports from Chloe's household about divisions in the church
(1:11–17).

It's generally easy to spot a *narratio*, as it usually began with a
disclosure formula involving the idea of 'knowledge' and often
contained the Greek word *gar* ('for').[2] Here's how each *narratio*
begins in Paul's undisputed letters; note the consistency:[3]

- Romans 1:13: I do not want you to be unaware . . .
- 1 Corinthians 1:11: For it has been reported to me concerning
  you . . .
- 2 Corinthians 1:8: For we do not want you to be ignorant . . .
- Galatians 1:11: For I make known to you . . .
- Philippians 1:12: And I want to make known to you . . .

---

2. Michael de Brauw, 'The Parts of the Speech', in Ian Worthington (ed.),
   A Companion to Greek Rhetoric (Malden, MA: Blackwell, 2007), p. 193.
3. My translations.

- Colossians 2:1: For I want you to know . . .
- 1 Thessalonians 1:4: We know . . .
- 1 Thessalonians 2:1: For you yourselves know . . .

Preaching from a *narratio*

The temptation when preaching from a *narratio* is to look for some kind of object lesson we can draw from the story – a similar temptation to that faced when preaching on Old Testament narrative. We look for a pattern of behaviour and then attempt to apply that pattern to the lives of our hearers.

For example, Paul's *narratio* in Galatians has been used to explore the notion of our own experience of divine revelation (1:15–16),[4] the importance of welcoming and affirming new converts with enthusiasm (1:22–24)[5] and to give a pattern for the conversion stories of all believers (1:11–24)[6] – but is any of this in line with the function of the text, or Paul's intent in narrating these events?

To answer that question, we need to keep in mind the function of a *narratio*: to define and frame the topic being addressed, and to do so in such a way as to start persuading the audience in favour of the speaker's case.

First, if the *narratio* is defining and framing the central issue, it should be our most fertile source of information about the rhetorical context. We can use it to exegete the original situation into which the author spoke, and begin to find similarities within our own situation into which the text might also speak today. In other words, rather than finding direct application, we lay the groundwork for

---

4. David K. Huttar, *Galatians: The Gospel According to Paul*, The Deeper Life Pulpit Commentary (Camp Hill: Christian Publications, 2001), pp. 39–40; cf. also Scot McKnight, *Galatians: From Biblical Text . . . to Contemporary Life*, NIV Application Commentary (Grand Rapids: Zondervan, 1995), p. 79.

5. Huttar, *Galatians*, pp. 42–43.

6. Eugene H. Peterson, *Traveling Light: Modern Meditations on St Paul's Letter of Freedom* (Colorado Springs: Helmers & Howard, 1988), pp. 45–55.

future application by looking at the similarities and differences between the world of the text and our own world.

In the *narratio* of 1 Corinthians (1:11–17), for example, two key aspects of the rhetorical situation are found: the Corinthians are divided over the various itinerant preachers, and Paul himself is refusing to 'play the game' by competing. This view of public speaking was common in the ancient world and was particularly acute in Corinth, with the wealthy trying to display their status by hosting the best speakers in their homes. We see that the church was simply adopting the values of the city around it, bringing the world's standards of judgment into the church (in this instance, judgments about rhetoric and social status). This gives us ample opportunity to explore similar problems in our own churches, whether it be division over preaching styles or over other sources of social 'branding' which we might bring into the church – often unconsciously and uncritically – from the culture around us. The purpose of our sermon, then, would be to show how Paul's message to the Corinthians can be just as much a word on target for our own situation.

We could do the same sort of thing with the Judaizing controversy narrated in Galatians 2, exploring how we're tempted to add external boundary markers as requirements of following Jesus. Alternatively, we might think about whether our own story as a believing community has anything in common with that of the Thessalonians (1 Thess. 1:4–10), who 'turned to God from idols' and welcomed the gospel in such a wholehearted way as to be an example to the other churches in the region. The first order of business with a *narratio* is to look at what we have in common with the original rhetorical situation – as well as what we don't.

Second, we need to preach the *narratio* in the light of the *propositio* (the main point of the speech). We'll talk more about the *propositio* in the next chapter – especially about how it helps us discern the function of every other part of the speech; but for now, all we need to know is that the *narratio* was intended to present the facts in the manner most favourable to the *propositio*. As we said before, it's a 'persuasive exposition'.[7] So if we can work out how the *narratio* is intending to

---

7. Quintilian, *Institutes of Oratory*, 4.2.21.

persuade the audience of the truth of the *propositio*, we can at least draw some preliminary application along those lines. Let's look at a couple of examples.

Returning briefly to the *narratio* of 1 Corinthians, we see that Paul narrates several facts in a way that supports the *propositio* 'be united' (1:10):

1. Their factionalism centred on different leaders is described using quotes that resemble political slogans.[8] It's painted as being foolish by the inclusion of the 'Christ faction', raising the absurd idea of Christ being divided (1:12–13). Paul also mocks their allegiance to leaders by asking if the leaders were the ones crucified for them, or the ones into whom they were baptized. Likewise, we could point out the absurdity of our divisions today, and ask if *our* Christian heroes and celebrities were crucified for us!

2. Paul narrates the fact that he didn't baptize many of the Corinthians in a very offhand way – even 'forgetting' precisely whom he baptized! He does this to emphasize that their primary allegiance should be to Christ, not to an individual leader. Our sermon, therefore, won't focus on a discussion of the theology of baptism in the abstract – or what it might have meant to baptize whole households – but on how baptism is *into Christ* and therefore should be a *source of unity*. The application is in line with the *propositio* about unity and the absence of factions.

In Philippians, the *narratio* (1:12–26) describes the fact that Paul is imprisoned at the time of writing. However, it spins it in such a way as to reinterpret this as being honourable, in contrast with his dishonourable opponents who were stirring up trouble for him out

8. So Larry L. Welborn, *Politics and Rhetoric in the Corinthian Epistles* (Macon, GA: Mercer University Press, 1997), p. 16; though note Margaret M. Mitchell, *Paul and the Rhetoric of Reconciliation* (Louisville: Westminster John Knox Press, 1993), pp. 83–85.

of envy and selfish motives. In telling the story, Paul draws out at least three key points:

1. The spread of the gospel is more important to him than any physical or social harm he might suffer (1:12–18);
2. He puts his hope for vindication in Christ (1:19–21);
3. He puts others' needs ahead of his own (1:22–26).

At each point, Paul is implicitly presenting himself as an example of what he explicitly calls the Philippians to do in the *propositio*: stand firm for the gospel as the number one priority despite any suffering it might entail (1:27), confident that Christ will vindicate (1:28). As they do this, they are to be united (1:27) – which Paul goes on to say is achieved through putting others first (2:4) in imitation of Christ (2:5). In this way, the *narratio* functions as an example of how the *propositio* is lived out in the life of the speaker. Our sermon, then, can use Paul's example as its basis for application.

Frank Thielman, in the NIV Application Commentary series, takes this line in applying Philippians 1. He uses it as an illustration of how valuable it can be to find examples of Christians who suffer the way a believer ought to. He acknowledges there isn't any 'direct command' to do this in the text, but from other cues in the letter (such as calls to imitate Paul in 3:17 and 4:9) he thinks '*it seems likely* that *part of his purpose* in recording these words for the Philippians is to provide them with an example for how they should think about their own hardships' (italics mine).[9] I agree. However, if we understand the role of the *narratio*, it's not just 'likely that [it's] part of his purpose', it's a *key function* of this part of a speech. That is, if we're applying the principles of rhetorical criticism, we can be more confident about Paul's purpose in writing, and develop application accordingly.

We'll next use this passage from Philippians in a sample sermon, providing one way of preaching this *narratio* in the light of the *propositio*.

---

9. Frank Thielman, *Philippians*, NIV Application Commentary (Grand Rapids: Zondervan, 1995), p. 65.

Summary: The *narratio*

Use the *narratio* to exegete the rhetorical situation, showing the similarities
with your own situation (as well as the differences).
Preach the *narratio* in the light of the *propositio*.

Exercise

1. How does the *narratio* of Romans (1:13–15) prepare the audience
for the *propositio* (1:16–17)?
2. What application, if any, would you draw from the *narratio*?

A SERMON ON A *NARRATIO*

This sermon on Philippians 1:12–30 was preached just before Australia Day in 2014 and draws on the strategies outlined in chapter 5. In particular, it preaches the narratio *in the light of the* propositio *(1:27–30), which is a call to live as good citizens (of heaven). The* propositio *gives us confidence that in the* narratio *Paul is exemplifying what it means to be specifically a good citizen, rather than just 'a good Christian' in a more general sense.*[10]

A good citizen of Australia

> Begin with the theme of 'good citizens' found in the *propositio*.

What does it mean to be a good citizen of Australia?

What makes us a good citizen of our country? The traditional answers are things like:

- Must eat Vegemite and at least *pretend* to like it, particularly around visiting Americans;
- Must know all the verses to 'Waltzing Matilda' – and both tunes;
- Must *not* know the second verse to our national anthem, 'Advance Australia Fair' – or, even better, not know that there *is* a second verse;
- Must rubbish New Zealanders at every opportunity – unless they become globally famous, in which case we make them honorary Australians (technically known as the 'Russell Crowe doctrine').[11]

---

10. Given the context in which I preached this sermon it was natural to use the idea of Australian citizenship as a starting point, but of course something similar could be done for any context.
11. For American readers, substitute 'Canadians' and you'll understand the dynamic.

They're the traditional stereotypes I grew up with. It's a little more complicated these days because Australian citizens come from all parts of the globe. We're a little harder to caricature. But still, we have some values that we *expect* of ourselves as citizens, even if we don't manage to live up to them all the time:

- We're the land of the 'fair go' – we expect everyone to be given an opportunity, and to work hard in response.
- We value 'mateship' and an egalitarian culture – this is one of the few countries in the world where it's perfectly normal for us to call our national leader by his or her first name rather than 'Prime Minister'.
- And, above all, we don't take ourselves too seriously, particularly when it comes to discussions about what makes a good citizen; so I'll stop there for fear of being called 'un-Australian'.

But it's clear that, however casual we might be when discussing it, there are certain responsibilities we have – certain values we need to embrace – if we're to be a good citizen of our country.

A good citizen of the empire

In Paul's day it wasn't much different.

Another time, another culture – but still there were values and responsibilities to being a good citizen of the Roman Empire: things like participating in civic festivals, civic religion; honouring the emperor, showing appropriate gratitude to benefactors.

> Explain citizenship in the first century.

And they took civic duty quite seriously – certainly more seriously than we do. They talked about it, wrote about it. There was a whole vocabulary associated with it. In the first century your duties as a good citizen were clear. Everyone knew what made a good citizen of Rome.

A good citizen of heaven

> Exegete the
> *propositio.*

Which is why there's a whole load of cultural freight attached when Paul says, in the theme statement of his letter to the Philippians, that his readers should be . . . *good citizens.*

We find this central proposition beginning in verse 27 of chapter 1; read it with me:

> Whatever happens, *conduct yourselves in a manner* worthy of the gospel
> of Christ. (1:27a)

And that emphasized phrase, 'conduct yourselves in a manner', is translating the Greek word *politeuomai.* It's from the technical vocabulary of citizenship. It means to live as a citizen of a city – you can see the word 'politics' is related to it. Paul is saying *be good citizens,* worthy of the gospel: something that would have resonated with the Philippians, given that they were one of only five Macedonian cities given citizenship by Rome.

But just in case you thought he was referring to *Roman* citizenship, a little later on in the letter he makes it clear that he's not. He's talking of an even *greater* citizenship. In contrast with those who live as if *this world,* as if *this existence,* is all there is, he says:

> But our citizenship is in heaven. And we eagerly await a Saviour from
> there, the Lord Jesus Christ. (3:20)

We have a citizenship of a greater order than that of Rome or Australia, one whose ideals and values must come before those of our earthly societies. And in this letter to the Philippians, Paul outlines the responsibilities and values of this citizenship. What makes a good citizen of heaven?

Let's look at the rest of Paul's theme statement, reading from verse 27 to the end of the chapter:

> Whatever happens, conduct yourselves in a manner worthy of the gospel
> of Christ. Then, whether I come and see you or only hear about you in

my absence, I will know that you stand firm in the *one Spirit, striving together as one* for the faith of the gospel without being frightened in any way by those who oppose you. This is a sign to them that *they will be destroyed, but that you will be saved* – and that by God. For it has been granted to you on behalf of Christ not only to believe in him, but also to *suffer* for him, since you are going through the same struggle you saw I had, and now hear that I still have. (1:27–30)

Clearly, good citizens of heaven are united.

No factions or quarrels like we see in Corinth. In fact, as we'll see in chapter 2 in a deservedly famous passage of Scripture, a good citizen's attitude to others should be the same as that of Christ Jesus: characterized by humility and putting others first.

> Show how the *propositio* plays out throughout the rest of the letter, in order to introduce the series.

Good citizens of heaven have a common purpose, which they strive towards regardless of personal suffering and personal cost. Later in the epistle we'll see the example of Timothy, who puts Jesus' interests ahead of his own. And the example of Epaphroditus, who Paul says almost died for the work of Christ.

Further, good citizens of heaven live their lives in the light of the age to come – in contrast with the Judaizers of chapter 3. Paul says that *they* have their mind set on earthly things – but *our* citizenship is in heaven, from where we eagerly await our Saviour.

So that's the central theme of Philippians: Paul's guide to gospel citizenship, introduced in those verses we just read.

But even before we get to verse 27, Paul's *already* been illustrating heavenly citizenship.

Even before we get to the examples of Jesus and Timothy and Epaphroditus – right from the beginning he uses his own example. He uses it to show what it means to be a good citizen of heaven – particularly when it's difficult; when acting as a citizen of heaven puts you in direct conflict with being a good

> Mention the rhetorical function of the *narratio* – how is Paul already seeking to persuade?

citizen of the world; when it involves *suffering* for the gospel.

So in the time we have left, we're going to look at what Paul's trying to tell us in chapter 1 about being a good citizen of heaven.

> For the rest of the sermon, show how Paul's example illustrates how to be a good citizen of heaven.

What can we learn from his example of being a gospel citizen in the face of opposition and hardship?

A good citizen of heaven asks not what my country can do for me . . .

The first characteristic of good citizens of heaven is this: they put Jesus and his gospel first. To borrow from JFK, they ask not what their country can do for them, but what they can do for their country. They put their own welfare second to the spread of the gospel. Have a listen to what Paul says:

> Now I want you to know, brothers and sisters, that what has happened to me has actually served to advance the gospel. As a result, it has become clear throughout the whole palace guard and to everyone else that I am in chains for Christ. And because of my chains, most of the brothers and sisters have become confident in the Lord and dare all the more to proclaim the gospel without fear. (1:12–14)

Now the Philippians were probably worried about Paul – after all, he's in chains, under house arrest. And they may even have been worried about the spread of the gospel – Paul's no longer running around the empire evangelizing. But he reassures them that this isn't a problem for God.

In fact, in the sovereignty of God, it's actually a *good* thing! Because all the soldiers have been stuck guarding Paul twenty-four hours a day, with nothing to do but talk. And what do you think they're going to talk about? The gospel, if Paul has any say in it!

You can imagine the scene. The soldier says, 'So, how come you're under arrest?' Paul says, 'I'm in chains because of this guy Jesus, who rose from the dead. Would you like me to tell you about him?' And in the absence of Angry Birds on his mobile, the soldier doesn't have anything better to do. So the apostle Paul shares the gospel with him for the duration of his watch. After a few weeks, the entire palace guard would have heard about Jesus!

No mere *imprisonment* can keep the gospel in chains! In fact, it's spread all the more because of Paul's suffering. All *Paul* had to do was wait for the inevitable questions and whip out his copy of *II Ways to Live* (that's the Roman edition).

In this, Paul gives us an example of what it means to be a citizen of heaven; an example of how *any* situation we're in – no matter how bad – can be used by God to advance the gospel.

Now hang on, you say, it's all fine for Paul. In chains for preaching the gospel – that's a pretty good conversation starter. But how does it work *for me*? I'm not in chains for anything, let alone the gospel. How's this relevant in twenty-first-century Sydney?

It's like your typical world-famous evangelist trying to explain to the rest of us how it's done. Because *his* examples usually involve sitting next to a business traveller on a plane as he heads off to speak at a Christian conference. By the time the first round of drinks has been served, he's answered the 'where are you off to' question and smoothly transitioned into talking about Jesus. By the time the wheels touch down, he's led most of business class to Christ, as well as three stewardesses and a would-be terrorist who has now vowed to use his remaining Semtex for good and not evil. 'See how God can use an ordinary person like me!' he exclaims.

Meanwhile, back in the real world, we're left wondering how those of us who *aren't* keynote speakers can move beyond talking about sport, the kids and the current body shape of celebrities.

It's easier for those of us in full-time ministry, too. People invariably ask you what your job is, so we can go from there. Particularly when people say, 'What would you want to do *that* for – couldn't you earn lots more money doing something else?' I'm not in prison for the gospel, but I did give up a career. And people are curious as to why I'd do that.

But for everyone: if you're putting the gospel first, surely there's *something* you've given up for it! You're not imprisoned. You're probably not facing intense persecution. But what have you given up? Try to bring the conversation around to those things, and see where it leads.

When I was a youth leader, back in the last millennium, I gave up my Friday nights. It wasn't all that hard to let people know that's where I was off to after a hard week at work. And many times people would ask me why I'd do that. And it gave me a great chance to explain.

For those who are in the secular workforce: off you go to church on Sunday morning – you give up your Sunday sleep-ins. Monday morning, when you get the obligatory 'What did you do at the weekend?', be bold and mention church. 'Hey, you don't actually give money to those preachers, do you?' 'Yes, I joyfully support the work of the gospel. Let me tell you why . . .'

If we put the gospel first, and suffer even in some tiny way because of it, others will take notice. They might even listen to what we say. Our *suffering* for the gospel, even on a small scale, can be used powerfully by God to advance the gospel.

Now Paul gives a second example, which we haven't got time to look at, but it essentially makes the same point. Some were preaching the gospel, he says, from 'false motives' – trying to stir up trouble for Paul while he was imprisoned. But still, he says, the end result is good for the gospel. And so he rejoices.

> But what does it matter? The important thing is that in every way, whether from false motives or true, Christ is preached. And because of this I rejoice. (1:18)

We rejoice whenever living for Christ becomes costly – because we know that the gospel will advance regardless. More than that – because we know that God can use *even our suffering*, great or small, to advance the gospel.

We have confidence in God's sovereignty; that he's in control, and he knows what he's doing. Which leads to the second characteristic we see in Paul.

A good citizen of heaven is confident of being vindicated
Citizens of heaven are confident: confident that, ultimately, the gospel will be vindicated – and we too along with it. That's how Paul continues:

> Yes, and I will continue to rejoice, for I know that through your prayers and God's provision of the Spirit of Jesus Christ what has happened to

me *will turn out for my deliverance*. I eagerly expect and hope that I will in
no way be ashamed, but will have sufficient courage so that now as always
Christ will be exalted in my body, whether by life or by death. (1:18b–20)

Paul believes that his circumstances, all that has happened to him,
'will turn out for his deliverance'. Not necessarily his physical deliverance from *prison* – as verse 20 suggests that's still unknown; but
more the idea of deliverance as *vindication*. Because what Paul's doing
here is alluding to the words of Job:

Indeed, this will turn out for my deliverance. (Job 13:16)

Like Paul, Job suffered even though he hadn't done anything
wrong – which damaged his reputation in the eyes of his community.
Even his friends thought he must have committed some sin and got
what was coming to him.

But Job was convinced that he'd done nothing to deserve it. He
was intent on being declared innocent by God – on being vindicated
in front of his family and friends. And, at the end of the story, Job
is indeed vindicated before God, and in the court of public opinion.

Paul quotes this because it's very similar to his own situation. He's
convinced that, despite what's happened to him, he'll be vindicated
like Job. He'll be proven to be in the right. Not necessarily in the
human court of public opinion, but before the heavenly court, which
is the only one that counts.

Job didn't know of an afterlife in heaven with God, so he yearned
for vindication while still alive. Paul – and we – know that there is a
court where ultimate vindication takes place, and it's *that* which he
yearns for.

Yet he's also keen to be vindicated here and now, if at all possible.
Not for his own sake, of course, but for the sake of the gospel which
he preaches. He might still lose the court case and be put to death,
but he'll have his chance in Rome to give the same kind of defence
of the gospel he gave in Jerusalem in Acts 22, to Governor Felix in
Acts 24 and to King Agrippa in Acts 26.

The very fact that he's appealed to the emperor and has the
chance to give a defence means he's already won. He's *confident* that
this will turn out for the vindication of his gospel.

What about us, when we face opposition, ridicule – from opponents of the gospel? Some of us from family? Friends? People we used to work with?

For a start, we rejoice, because we know that we'll ultimately be vindicated in the eyes of the only one who counts – God.

But we also remain eager for vindication here and now. Not for *ourselves* to be vindicated – although it's nice if that happens – but for the *gospel* to be vindicated. Like Paul, we take *every* opportunity we're given to defend God and his gospel.

Because if we are indeed putting the gospel first, if we are being good citizens of the gospel, then that's what matters – even more than life itself.

A good citizen of heaven knows that living is Christ and dying is gain

Which leads us to Paul's famous statement:

> For to me, to live is Christ and to die is gain. (1:21)

In other words, living means experiencing Christ and working for the spread of his gospel. His singular passion; his focus in life.

And what's the worst that can happen to him? Death? Ha! That's actually *gain*. Or, as he goes on to say a few verses later, it's *better by far!* Bring it on!

It's often said that life begins at forty. For years I wondered whether that was true. I'm forty-one now. It's not. Turns out it was just a sad delusion of the baby-boomer generation. But it's no delusion for Christians to say that life begins at death. Dying is *gain*.

Now, we pay lip service to this, but do we really believe it? If we were given the choice right now, would we *really* choose to leave our comfortable life and be with Christ? I don't know about you, but most of the Christians I hang out with, if they're honest, they have a hard time really believing that. Much of the time *I* live as if I don't really believe it either. To die is *gain*?

Leave aside the dying bit for a minute: what about the living? For us, is living *really* Christ? Are we *really* consumed with Christ and his gospel? Or for us is living really Christ plus something else? This is how Gordon Fee puts it: 'Too often for us it is "for me to live is Christ – plus work, leisure, accumulating wealth, relationships" etc. And if the truth were known, all too often the "plus factor" has become our primary passion.'[12]

Paul's example chastens us, doesn't it? But it's the secret of how he's content, how he's joyful, even in the midst of the most trying of circumstances: because his life is all about Christ and his gospel. It's his passion; his reason for living. And because he knows that death isn't the end.

But despite this, Paul isn't planning on dying just yet. Although his *desire* is to be with Christ, he's convinced he'll remain for the time being: because God has a job for him to do.

> If I am to go on living in the body, this will mean fruitful labour for me. Yet what shall I choose? I do not know! I am torn between the two: I desire to depart and be with Christ, which is better by far; but it is more necessary for you that I remain in the body. Convinced of this, I know that I will remain, and I will continue with all of you for your progress and joy in the faith, so that through my being with you again your boasting in Christ Jesus will abound on account of me. (1:22–26)

Back when my eldest son was four, as I was putting him to bed one night, we started talking about heaven. After a while, he asked a very logical question. He said, 'Well, if heaven's so good, why can't we just go there now?' How do you answer that?

Well, we'd just done Rick Warren's *40 Days of Purpose* as a church, so I gave a response that I thought would surely put me in the running for Purpose-Driven Dad ™ of the Year. I told him about having a purpose here on earth. God's put us here for the purpose of telling others about Jesus. That's why we're here.

I'll never forget the look on his face – eyes wide in complete and utter disbelief. 'But *I* thought we were here to play with *toys*?'

And when you're four years old, that's pretty much your purpose in life, isn't it? Trouble is, many of us don't grow out of that. Many

---

12. Gordon Fee, *Philippians*, New International Commentary on the New Testament (Grand Rapids: Eerdmans, 1995), p. 150.

in the church don't grow out of that. To live is to play with toys, and Christ is just my death insurance.

But, in reality, we're here on borrowed time. It *is* better for us to depart now and be with Christ – better by far. But, for some reason, God thinks it's more necessary for each of us to remain. Why? Because he has a purpose for us:

- To be good citizens of heaven while remaining here, where God has placed us;
- To ask what we can do for the gospel, for it to advance;
- To be confident that the gospel will be vindicated, and us along with it.

And to follow Paul's example in being single-minded about that purpose. So are you going to play with toys for the rest of your life? Or will you say, along with Paul, 'For me, living is Christ, and dying is gain'?

6. PROPOSITIO

Ideally, each sermon is the explanation, interpretation or application of a single dominant idea supported by other ideas, all drawn from one passage or several passages of Scripture.[1]

Many preachers have been trained to craft a sermon around one 'big idea', as Haddon Robinson famously put it. Every other part of the sermon should operate in support of that central idea; if it doesn't, it belongs in another sermon.

This principle is not unique to preaching, but can be found in good rhetoric across cultures and throughout the ages. Graeco-Roman rhetoric of the first century was no exception. The 'big idea' was called the *propositio* – the main proposition or idea the speaker was trying to communicate. All the other parts of the speech served, in some way, to argue in favour of this *propositio*.

Sometimes there was more than one part to the *propositio*. In this case it was often called a *partitio* or *divisio*, as it outlined the major

---

1. Haddon W. Robinson, *Biblical Preaching: The Development and Delivery of Expository Messages*, 2nd edn (Grand Rapids: Baker Academic, 2001), p. 35.

divisions of the speech, often in the order they'd be presented. This prepared the audience for the sequence of ideas that would follow.

In fact, that was the purpose of this part of the speech. It was the PowerPoint presentation of the ancient world, making the structure of the speech clear to the audience. Cicero says that 'an arrangement of the subjects to be mentioned in an argument, when properly made, renders the whole oration clear and intelligible'.[2] Its purpose was to aid both clarity and memorability, telling the audience in advance what the speech was about and what it was trying to *do*.

Preaching from a *propositio*

I recall hearing preacher and commentary writer David Jackman speaking about preaching the epistles. He referred to the great 'pearls' in the New Testament – the individual chapters, paragraphs or arguments. He said that the secret to interpreting these pearls is to discern the reason each one is precisely where it is: to find 'the string upon which all the pearls hang', as I recall him putting it. What's the thread that runs through an epistle that makes all of its parts hang together?

Rhetorical theory tells us that the answer to that question – at least in part – is found in the *propositio*. For preaching, this is the most important part of the speech – for three reasons. First, it defines the rhetorical function of the epistle as a whole. Second, it acts as a hermeneutical control over every other part of the epistle. And, third, in the case of a more developed *partitio*, it provides a handy way of preaching an overview of the entire epistle. We'll look at each of these points in turn. (And this paragraph, by the way, is a *partitio*.)

The rhetorical function
First, the *propositio* tells us the rhetorical function of the entire epistle: what it's about and what it's trying to do. It tells us how to apply the letter as a whole. This is best illustrated by some examples.

---

2. Cicero, *On Invention*, 1.22.

1 Corinthians

> I appeal to you, brothers and sisters, in the name of our Lord Jesus
> Christ, that all of you agree with one another in what you say and
> that there be no divisions among you, but that you be perfectly united in
> mind and thought. (1 Cor. 1:10)

This *propositio* is found just after the *exordium*. It's an appeal to
concord and harmony, in the light of the division described in the
narratio (1:11–17) – the 'I follow Paul, I follow Apollos' bit that
comes next.

Philippians

> Whatever happens, conduct yourselves in a manner [*politeuomai*] worthy
> of the gospel of Christ. Then, whether I come and see you or only hear
> about you in my absence, I will know that you stand firm in the one
> Spirit, striving together as one for the faith of the gospel without being
> frightened in any way by those who oppose you. This is a sign to them
> that they will be destroyed, but that you will be saved – and that by God.
> For it has been granted to you on behalf of Christ not only to believe in
> him, but also to suffer for him, since you are going through the same
> struggle you saw I had, and now hear that I still have. (Phil. 1:27–30)

The *propositio* of Philippians comes straight after Paul's *narratio* about
his imprisonment. It's an appeal to civic-mindedness (Paul uses the
citizenship word *politeuomai*) and unity within the church in the midst
of suffering. This is to be achieved by imitating the examples of
both Paul-in-chains (already mentioned in the *narratio*) and Christ
crucified (the first argument, 2:1–11).

Romans

> For I am not ashamed of the gospel, because it is the power of God
> that brings salvation to everyone who believes: first to the Jew, then to
> the Gentile. For in the gospel the righteousness of God is revealed –
> a righteousness that is by faith from first to last, just as it is written:
> 'The righteous will live by faith.' (Rom. 1:16–17)

The *propositio* is again where we'd expect to find it – just after the *narratio* about why Paul is writing (1:13–15). Despite its complexity, Romans is fundamentally an argument for Jew–Gentile equality based on the righteousness-by-faith nature of the gospel.

In sum, rather than needing to speculate about the unifying theme or themes of an epistle, rhetorical theory *tells us* where to find the central purpose: in the *propositio*.

A hermeneutical control

Since the *propositio* defines what the epistle is about, it then acts as a hermeneutical control over the rest of the epistle. That is, we can work out the function of *every other passage* we preach from by seeing how it contributes to proving the *propositio*. This helps narrow down our options of what a text might be doing. We could put it in diagram form:

Purpose of the epistle in the *propositio* → Function of every other part

For example, as I said earlier, 1 Corinthians 13 has an epideictic function. It praises the virtue of selfless love in order to encourage the audience to love all the more. This, however, is just the small picture. The *reason* Paul wants the Corinthians to embrace selfless love is because of the bigger picture of the epistle – the deliberative aim of encouraging unity in the church. It's not about selfless love in isolation, but selfless love *as a means to Christian unity*.

So a sermon on 1 Corinthians 13 should do likewise. It should also praise selfless love in order to encourage our hearers to love all the more, but the explicit context and purpose of this love should be to produce a united fellowship: we tie it in to Paul's overall aim. In the same way, a sermon on the next chapter (1 Cor. 14) shouldn't primarily be a treatise on tongues and prophecy – along the lines of 'Everything You've Ever Wanted to Ask about Speaking in Tongues But Were Afraid to Ask (In Case There Wasn't an Interpreter Present)'. Instead, it should focus on how spiritual gifts should be used in a way that promotes unity instead of division. Why? Because that's what Paul's doing with it! More broadly, every sermon in 1 Corinthians should at least be framed by this issue of unity, showing how the particular content of the passage in question contributes to Paul's appeal for unity.

Now this may in some cases feel quite restrictive – and, if we're serious about respecting the original intent, it may need to be! Yet it can also open up areas of application which might traditionally have been overlooked. Some arguments in Paul's epistles may at first glance seem to be dry points of theology. We might feel as if all our sermon can 'do' is to get people to agree with it, or to remind them that they do in fact already agree with it. However, when we investigate the rhetorical function of the particular theological point being made – how it relates to the *propositio* – we may see some application in the light of that broader rhetorical function.

Let's recap another example from chapter 2. Although there are sections of Romans 1 – 8 which present aspects of the doctrine of grace, the overriding purpose is found in the *propositio* (1:16–17). Again, this purpose speaks to a unity within the church that transcends human divisions (such as race and culture). The doctrine that 'all have sinned' is important to grasp in its own right; but in the context of the whole epistle it also functions as a reminder that *because* we have all sinned, none of us is any 'better' than anyone else. We're all sinners saved by grace. In this way, doctrine has an immediate, social outworking in the community of believers.

This kind of restrictive focus also goes some way to preventing what I think is a common preaching error: the simplistic identification of a 'topic' within the passage, followed by what is a generic, 'topical' sermon on that passage – with the predictable, generic application on that topic. A sermon on 1 Corinthians 13 ought not be an excuse for the preacher's favourite stories and truisms about love: it's primarily about love as an antidote for a divided Christian community. There may well be application to other spheres of life – such as marriage, family and the workplace – but this is secondary and should be noted as such.

An objection to this, of course, is that application from week to week over a long-running series can become very similar. (Hopefully this would only be at a macro-level, as each text is wonderfully unique.) This highlights one of the problems with taking a text which was originally to be delivered as a unified speech arguing for one central proposition, and turning it into a six-month teaching programme (or, in the famous case of Martyn Lloyd-Jones, much, much longer).

Now your church might *need* to focus on unity for half a year. If they don't, though, there's a lot of ways to avoid repetition. You could deal with larger amounts of text at a time; or break up a preaching series on a longer epistle into smaller series over a number of years; or focus only on some key sections. Nevertheless, if each sermon is to *do* what its section of biblical text *did*, its primary function must be to support the *propositio*, even if sometimes that can get a bit repetitive.

To look at this from a more positive angle, a conscious use of the *propositio* over the duration of a preaching series can help to cement the central idea in our congregation's consciousness. Ideally, at the end of such a series the congregation should be able to explain the *propositio* in their own words, and see how the whole series related to it. Perhaps the *propositio* could even form a congregational 'memory verse' for the duration, old-fashioned as the practice may now seem!

Sidenote: what about secondary application?

I should point out here that I'm not arguing against secondary application, but I think we ought to identify it *as* secondary and therefore be more cautious. When looking for guidance in areas not directly addressed by Scripture, it may be right to develop *inferences* from some aspect or other of the text, but these inferences only inform our wisdom, and aren't of the same order as the explicit or implicit teaching that's in line with the text's rhetorical intent.

My practice is to tell my congregation the point at which I'm moving beyond the original rhetorical intent and to use more cautious language: 'this suggests' rather than 'the Bible says'. I also tend to be more brief with these secondary applications, so they don't overshadow the main function of the text. (And I often physically move to one side as I deal with it, flagging it as an aside.) One example of this might be the implications of Paul's statements about original sin (Rom. 5:12–21) for babies who die in the womb or before they reach the 'age of accountability' (whenever that might be). This is a subject that for pastoral reasons needs to be addressed, but it's clearly a long way from Paul's rhetorical intent in Romans 5.

We also need to be sure that any secondary application we derive is not at odds with the explicit rhetorical intent. And there has to be *some* degree of similarity with the original situation being addressed, otherwise our secondary application has become an exercise in proof-texting.

Preaching an overview sermon

As well as defining the rhetorical function of the epistle and interpreting its individual parts, a longer *propositio* can provide a 'window' onto the epistle as a whole. It can even give the basis of an overview sermon (like that suggested by Mark Dever, mentioned already in chapter 4). Epistles suited to this kind of treatment include Philippians (1:27–30), Colossians (2:6–15)[3] and Galatians (2:15–21), perhaps along with Paul's recap and expansion of his *propositio* in Romans 3:21–31.

Next, we'll workshop Galatians to see how such an overview sermon might be constructed.

Workshop: an overview of Galatians

The *partitio* of Galatians is found just after the extensive *narratio*, in 2:15–21. We'll read it now, with some brief commentary. Note that it's presented as a summary of how Paul rebuked Peter over a previous situation in Antioch, which was analogous to what was happening in Galatia. And he begins with what should be common ground for all believers, whether Jew or Gentile:

> We who are Jews by birth and not sinful Gentiles know that a person is not justified by the works of the law, but by faith in Jesus Christ. So we, too, have put our faith in Christ Jesus that we may be justified by faith

---

3. For an excellent analysis of the *partitio*, see Barth L. Campbell, 'Colossians 2:6–15 as a Thesis: A Rhetorical-Critical Study', *Journal for the Study of Rhetorical Criticism of the New Testament*, <http://rhetjournal.net/RhetJournal/Articles_files/Campbell.pdf>, accessed 22 January 2016.

in Christ and not by the works of the law, because by the works of the law no one will be justified. (2:15–16)

That is, we all agree that justification doesn't come through the law. We're right with God, not by observing the Torah, but by our faith in Jesus (or, I think more likely, by the faithfulness *of* Jesus). Paul then moves on to what *is* in dispute: namely, does the absence of the law promote sin?

But if, in seeking to be justified in Christ, we Jews find ourselves also among the sinners, doesn't that mean that Christ promotes sin? Absolutely not! If I rebuild what I destroyed, then I really would be a law-breaker. (2:17–18)

He asks the question: What happens if we pursue right standing with God through Christ, not the law, and this results in 'finding ourselves also among the sinners'?[4] Does this make Christ a 'promoter' of sinful behaviour? No way! In fact, to go back to observing the law would be the sinful thing to do!

For through the law I died to the law so that I might live for God. I have been crucified with Christ and I no longer live, but Christ lives in me. The life I now live in the body, I live by faith in the Son of God, who loved me and gave himself for me. (2:19–20)

The reason Paul gives for dispensing with the law is that something new has happened: Christ living in the believer. Christ-in-me does away with the need for the law, enabling me to do that which is pleasing to God.

---

4. There are at least three possibilities for what Paul means by this phrase: discovering just how sinful we are, having been stripped of the law's restraint; becoming, in the eyes of law-observing Jews, 'sinners' just like the lawless Gentiles; or no longer having the law to function as a restraint on our behaviour. But this exegetical issue is peripheral to our task here.

I do not set aside the grace of God, for if righteousness could be gained through the law, Christ died for nothing! (2:21)

In conclusion, if we could be right with God through the law, there would have been no point in the death of Jesus.

We could summarize the key elements of the *partitio* as shown in Table 1.

Table 1: The key elements of the *partitio* in Galatians 2:15–21

2:15–16	(1) Justification does not come through the law.
2:17–18	(2) But does the absence of the law promote sin? No! To go back to reliance on the law would be sinful.
2:19–20	(3) Christ-in-me does away with the need for the law; my sinful nature has been crucified with Christ.
2:21	(4) To insist otherwise negates the need for Christ.

Exercise

Read through the rest of the proof section of Galatians (3:1 – 6:10). This will take a bit of time! For each argument (see divisions in the nearby table), note down how it supports an element of the *partitio* as given above. Possible answers are given on the next page.

Argument	How does it support an element of the *partitio*?
3:1–18	
3:19 – 4:7	
4:8–20	
4:21 – 5:1	
5:2–12	
5:13–26	
6:1–10	

Argument	How does it support an element of the *partitio*?[5]
3:1–18	Supports (1). Abraham was made right with God by faith, which came well before the law was added.
3:19 – 4:7	Supports (1). Why was the law given? The law was added as a restraining influence, but is no longer needed, as it has been replaced by something greater.
4:8–20	Supports (2). Going back to the law would be like going back to another form of slavery (exchanging slavery to pagan spirits for slavery to the law).
4:21 – 5:1	Supports (2). An allegory from history, arguing that those who rely on Christ are the true descendants of Isaac; to remain under the law is now to be a descendant of Ishmael!
5:2–12	Supports (4). The justification offered through Christ is nullified if we now rely on the law instead.
5:13–26	Supports (3). Christ-in-me (the Spirit) ensures that though we are without the law, we do not behave 'lawlessly'. We live according to the Spirit, not according to the works of the flesh.
6:1–10	Supports (3). Christ-in-me is also Christ-in-us: the restraining influence of a Spirit-filled community, which is the 'law' of Christ.

Getting practical

Once you've done this exercise, plan an overview sermon on Galatians 2:15–21. What material could you draw in from the rest of the epistle? (Think about using some of the stories of Abraham, Sarah and Hagar as illustrations.)

One more example

Before we finish this workshop, look back at the table in the exercise. Notice how this helps us see the kind of hermeneutical control the *partitio* has over the rest of the epistle. The purpose of every section

---

5. Tim MacBride, *Preaching the New Testament as Rhetoric: The Promise of Rhetorical Criticism for Expository Preaching*, Australian College of Theology Monograph Series (Eugene: Wipf & Stock, 2014), p. 118.

of text is to support an element of the *partitio*. Our sermons, then, should apply these texts in the light of their bigger function, rather than in isolation.

For example, the famous 'fruit of the Spirit' passage (Gal. 5:22–26) in the wider context isn't an isolated list of virtues which a Christian ought to display. Scot McKnight describes this as a 'slightly misguided' approach in which preachers 'focus on the individual dimensions of the fruit of the Spirit and . . . make this list a character-building piece of instruction'.[6] When preached this way, it can almost become a new law to strive to live up to.

Here in Galatians, though, the list functions as an argument for the superiority of the Spirit over the law in restraining sin. So our sermon application shouldn't simply be: be more loving, be more joyful, be more peacemaking and so on. It should be about the benefits of relying on Christ (not on the law or human effort) to restrain our sinful desires. They've been crucified with him, and in their place his Spirit fills us, producing these virtues (and others) as its fruit.

Of course, there's still the implication to live out these values. Paul reminds us not to use our freedom to indulge the sinful nature (5:13); rather, we should live by the Spirit (5:25). This command, however, is not an isolated abstraction but flows out of the primary theological point made back in the *partitio* (2:19–20).

And this is what we do with each element of the *probatio*, applying it in the light of how it supports the *propositio*.

Summary: Preaching the *propositio* . . .

The *propositio* is the thesis statement of a speech. It determines the function of the whole epistle and therefore:
- It helps us determine the function of each part of the epistle;
- It acts as a hermeneutical control over the rest of the epistle.

The *partitio* (or *divisio*) outlines the arguments which follow.
It can therefore provide the basis of an overview sermon, showing how the parts of the epistle work together.

---

6. Scot McKnight, *Galatians: From Biblical Text . . . to Contemporary Life*, NIV Application Commentary (Grand Rapids: Zondervan, 1995), p. 277.

7. REFUTATIO

Now you may be thinking, 'Hey, what happened to the *probatio* – didn't that come next?' Well, yes, you're right. In fact, it's so important it gets three chapters all to itself in part 3, where we look at the three different types of proof. But thanks for your question, as it gave me the opportunity to illustrate dealing with imagined objections. And that's what the *refutatio* was all about.

Or rather, that's *one* aspect of it. According to one of the ancient handbooks, *refutatio* was 'the method by which you anticipate and demolish the objections which can be brought against your speech'.[1] Fredrick Long has identified four purposes of *refutatio* in ancient speeches,[2] each of which we can find in the New Testament, and especially in Paul.

---

1. *Rhetoric for Alexander*, 33.
2. Fredrick J. Long, *Ancient Rhetoric and Paul's Apology: The Compositional Unity of 2 Corinthians*, Society for New Testament Studies Monograph Series (Cambridge: Cambridge University Press, 2004), p. 89.

- First, it was to counter opponents' arguments directly:

  > But if it is preached that Christ has been raised from the dead, how can some of you say that there is no resurrection of the dead? If there is no resurrection of the dead, then not even Christ has been raised. And if Christ has not been raised, our preaching is useless and so is your faith. (1 Cor. 15:12–14)

  > Why not say – as some slanderously claim that we say – 'Let us do evil that good may result'? Their condemnation is just! (Rom. 3:8)

- Second, it was to attack opponents by portraying their character and motivations in a bad light:

  > Those who want to impress people by means of the flesh are trying to compel you to be circumcised. The only reason they do this is to avoid being persecuted for the cross of Christ. Not even those who are circumcised keep the law, yet they want you to be circumcised that they may boast about your circumcision in the flesh. (Gal. 6:12–13)

  > In their greed these teachers will exploit you with fabricated stories. Their condemnation has long been hanging over them, and their destruction has not been sleeping. (2 Pet. 2:3)

- Third, it was to anticipate objections and counter-arguments:

  > But someone will ask, 'How are the dead raised? With what kind of body will they come?' How foolish! What you sow does not come to life unless it dies. (1 Cor. 15:35–36)

  > What shall we say, then? Shall we go on sinning, so that grace may increase? By no means! We are those who have died to sin; how can we live in it any longer? (Rom. 6:1–2)

- And, fourth, it was to answer criticism:

  > This is my defence to those who sit in judgment on me . . . (1 Cor. 9:3)

> If we are 'out of our mind', as some say, it is for God; if we are in
> our right mind, it is for you. (2 Cor. 5:13)

> For some say, 'His letters are weighty and forceful, but in person he
> is unimpressive and his speaking amounts to nothing.' Such people
> should realise that what we are in our letters when we are absent,
> we will be in our actions when we are present. (2 Cor. 10:10–11)

Sometimes, Paul's *refutatio* can be quite lengthy: in Romans 9 – 11
he refutes arguments (real or anticipated) among Gentile believers
in Rome.[3] He often uses the technique of diatribe (e.g. Rom. 3:1–8),
full of rhetorical questions, objections from imaginary dialogue
partners, and *apostrophes* (sudden addresses to an imagined audience
member – often a stereotype – which is 'overheard' by the audience,
to rhetorical effect).[4]

Preaching *refutatio*

So how can identifying *refutatio* in this way help us in preaching? Glad
you asked, O imaginary dialogue partner! I think there are at least
three ways this informs our preaching.

Hypothetical objections

Actually, the first isn't strictly about *preaching*, but about the foundational exegetical work. The fact that it was common to anticipate
possible arguments means we need to be cautious about assuming the
arguments were real. Many commentaries have built up pictures of
'Paul's opponents' without grappling with the possibility that Paul
was anticipating a hypothetical objection. After all, in a written-down
speech delivered by proxy, you couldn't answer hecklers on the spot;

---

3. See Ben Witherington III and Darlene Hyatt, *Paul's Letter to the
   Romans: A Socio-Rhetorical Commentary* (Grand Rapids: Eerdmans,
   2004), p. 237.
4. See Stanley Kent Stowers, *A Rereading of Romans: Justice, Jews, and
   Gentiles* (New Haven: Yale University Press, 1994).

you needed to anticipate the questioning that might occur – either out loud or in people's minds – and respond.

Similar objections in the twenty-first century

Since *refutatio* sections of the epistles answer objections to their arguments – both actual and anticipated – our preaching should consider *similar* objections which might be raised today. These may be explicit or implicit objections to God's Word made by the media, other religions, academia and so on. Alternatively, they may be objections raised by other Christian groups – even members of our own congregation – to the particular teaching in our scriptural text.

If they were *actual objections* in the original setting, think about who was doing the objecting. Then ask: Who occupies that same place in our contemporary setting? For example, in 2 Corinthians 10 Paul refers to 'some' (that is, real people) who were objecting to the way he went about his ministry. They didn't like his refusal to play the world's games of rhetoric, sophistication and status, instead using a different set of 'weapons' to advance the gospel:

> By the humility and gentleness of Christ, I appeal to you – I, Paul, who
> am 'timid' when face to face with you, but 'bold' towards you when away!
> I beg you that when I come I may not have to be as bold as I expect to
> be towards some people who think that we live by the standards of this
> world. For though we live in the world, we do not wage war as the world
> does. The weapons we fight with are not the weapons of the world.
> On the contrary, they have divine power to demolish strongholds.
> We demolish arguments and every pretension that sets itself up against
> the knowledge of God, and we take captive every thought to make it
> obedient to Christ. (2 Cor. 10:1–5)

In preaching this (admittedly difficult) text, first ask: Who in our own context would be like Paul's opponents? Identify the attitude we sometimes find in our churches (or even in ourselves) that encourages us to promote Christ using the tried-and-trusted strategies of our own culture – things like slick advertising, 'customer' focus and an appeal to felt needs. Then use the way Paul insists on other-worldly weapons to 'demolish' that argument!

If there were *actual opponents* whose behaviour the text calls out, call out that behaviour in our own world, too. Think about Galatians, where several times Paul presents the character and motivations of his (real) opponents in a bad light. Here's one such case:

> Those people are zealous to win you over, but for no good. What they want is to alienate you from us, so that you may have zeal for them. (Gal. 4:17)

Again, think about who might occupy the place of the Judaizers in our own setting – people who add extra requirements or behavioural markers to the gospel. Show how their motives for doing so can also be self-serving, even if unconsciously. Then also ask who might occupy the place of the 'foolish Galatians' who are tempted to go along with it – and *why*.

If, however, we're dealing with *anticipated objections* to an argument, ask whether these objections might still be raised by people in our own setting. For example, people might still logically (but incorrectly) conclude from Paul's teaching that grace gives us licence to continue sinning (Rom. 6:1, 15). And others might still equally logically (and equally incorrectly) decide that at least a measure of legalism is desirable so that grace does not lead to licentiousness. Both strands of objections are probably implied in Romans 6.

In either case, having identified similar objections in the world of our own hearers, try using the strategies found in the *refutatio* passage to guide your response to these objections. Look to the text to see if it gives a culturally appropriate way to answer these objections today. Other times, we might need to change or supplement the argument for our twenty-first-century audience (we'll look at an example of this shortly, in our workshop on 1 Corinthians 15, where Paul appeals to the practice of being baptized for the dead).

Different objections in the twenty-first century

Moving beyond the specific objections – real or anticipated – that were raised in the text, we can apply the principle that lies behind *refutatio*. That is, we can also look for *different* objections which might be raised today, whether by society in general or by our hearers specifically. We don't simply try to copy Paul's *lines* of anticipated refutation; we employ the *principle itself* of anticipating objections.

This is similar to a step in David Buttrick's preaching model which involves identifying potential stumbling blocks that might prevent the audience accepting the idea being preached.[5] Buttrick suggests this as a possible strategy for *any* text; I agree, but think it should be especially the case for texts that are all about refutation.

Enough theory. Let's look at how this might play out in a sermon on a *refutatio* text.

Workshop: preaching *refutatio* in 1 Corinthians 15

1 Corinthians 15 is an extended *refutatio*. At issue is the apostolic teaching of a bodily resurrection for believers. However, we find this out only once Paul starts answering objections, because in the first eleven verses Paul lays out the essence of the gospel proclamation. It centres on the *resurrected* Christ and is essential for salvation. So to reject this teaching leads to disadvantage (v. 2, using the terminology of deliberative rhetoric, 'you have believed *in vain*'). To support his point, Paul starts off with the positive argument: that Jesus' resurrection has been witnessed by others, and their testimony has been reliably passed down. He also mentions his own confirming testimony.

Then in verse 12 Paul raises the first objection to this teaching. It's clearly an actual objection since he asks, 'how can *some of you say* that there is no resurrection of the dead?' Notice that it's not really an objection to the teaching about *Jesus'* resurrection, but to the resurrection of the dead in general. The previous proof of Jesus' resurrection just laid the foundation for Paul's rebuttal: if there's no resurrection of the dead, then Jesus didn't rise from the dead – and that's essential to our faith! So if we throw *that* out, we've been wasting our time all along.

Later in the chapter, he raises a follow-up question relating to the bodily nature of the resurrection. It's introduced in verse 35 by

---

5. David Buttrick, *Homiletic: Moves and Structures* (Philadelphia: Fortress, 1987), p. 47.

the phrase 'But someone will ask', suggesting it's probably an anticipated objection (but we can't be sure).[6]

> But someone will ask, 'How are the dead raised? With what kind of body
> will they come?' (15:35)

He then goes on to answer this objection by discussing both
continuity and discontinuity between our present and resurrected
bodies.

Now, of course, there's a whole lot more going on in this chapter
that needs explanation if we're going to understand Paul's arguments
and preach them effectively. That's what commentaries are for. Here,
though, we're focusing on how our understanding of this chapter
as *refutatio* informs the function of our sermon: can we use the text
to do something in our world similar to what Paul intended it to do
in his world?

So how do we preach all of this?

First, we need to identify *who* in Paul's world was objecting to
the teaching about the bodily resurrection. Clearly it wasn't *all* of the
Corinthians, given the phrase 'some of you' (v. 12) and the fact that
others were being baptized for the dead (v. 29). Given that the bodily
resurrection was a feature of popular Judaism, it's most likely that
those objecting were Greeks. The very word for resurrection
(*anastasis*) sounds like the 'standing up of corpses'. This would have
been a new idea, and probably a ridiculous concept, in Greek
thought. It went against their ideas of the immortality of the soul
and the inferiority of the material world. The philosophers' scoffing
response to Paul's mention of the resurrection in Acts 17:31–32

---

6. Ben Witherington III sees it as part of the real situation: 'Apparently
   a major stumbling block – if not *the* stumbling block – for the
   Corinthians in accepting the notion of resurrection was that having
   a body seemed synonymous with mortality and corruptibility so that
   the combination of *body* and *immortality* did not make sense' (*Conflict
   and Community in Corinth: A Socio-Rhetorical Commentary on 1 and
   2 Corinthians* [Grand Rapids: Eerdmans, 1995], pp. 306–307).

gives further support to this reading.[7] Although it may be an anticipated objection, verse 35 also fits this scenario, as the question 'with
what kind of body?' hints at someone who views the material as
inferior.[8] The objection to a bodily resurrection arises most naturally
from the Greek philosophical worldview.

Unless you're preaching in a very niche church, your audience
today is unlikely to be comprised of Greek philosophers. Still,
many sections of Western society do have a similar reaction to the
idea of resurrection (bodily or otherwise) – or to any kind of
afterlife, for that matter.[9] It goes against the prevailing post-
Enlightenment, naturalistic view of the world. On the other hand,
people with other religious views may well embrace the idea of a
continued existence, but, just like the Greeks, think that the goal
is to *escape* the material. This is especially the case in Eastern
religions. Much of the world around us finds the idea of a bodily
resurrection as ridiculous as the Greeks did, which gives us our
main point of contact with Paul's strategy of *refutatio*. We then
bring Paul's arguments for bodily resurrection to bear in our
own setting.

Following the *principle* of anticipating objections, however, we
can go further – thinking about objections to Paul's teaching on the
resurrection which might not have been part of Paul's world. This
might include atheistic presuppositions (largely unknown in Paul's
day), a suspicion of history itself or even a mistrust of any kind
of metanarrative. We might even need to address questions raised
in the minds of believers in the light of more recent science, such
as the continuity of the self when the cells in our bodies are forever

---

7. Ibid., p. 302.

8. Ibid., p. 307.

9. See, as but one example, the blog of the atheist Sam Harris: 'People
   of faith tend to ignore the coming resurrection of the dead – perhaps
   because the idea is so obviously preposterous. And yet this is precisely
   the form of afterlife one must expect if one is to be a serious Jew,
   Christian or Muslim' ('Will the Dead Walk Again?', 31 March 2011,
   <http://www.samharris.org/blog/item/the-coming-resurrection-
   of-the-dead/2011>).

being replaced.[10] Paul's *refutatio* also needs to be directed at these objections that arise in our own day. And it may not be just to 'those outside' the faith, but increasingly to a believing congregation being constantly assailed by opposing worldviews.

In preaching Paul's *refutatio*, we also need to work out whether some of his arguments are still appropriate for our time and culture. Clearly the historically verifiable nature of Jesus' resurrection is central to Paul's argument and is just as valid today. The entire Christian faith (15:12–19) – both then and now – hinges on the fact of Christ's resurrection, and this should occupy a key position in our sermon. The greater historical distance might mean that we need to present more detailed evidence than Paul's brief creedal list of eyewitnesses.

Less relevant is his argument derived from the practice of being baptized for the dead (15:29), as it's not something being done in our churches today.[11] However, the idea *behind* this argument – appealing to a particular behaviour as evidence of belief in an afterlife – has contemporary parallels. Many of the things we humans do are, in the words of Peter Berger, 'signals of transcendence' and point to an innate hope within us that this is not all there is.[12] This gives us a further line of argument that's still in keeping with the

---

10. Ibid. Harris also raises the question of 'to whose body does it belong?' in regard to molecules which could have belonged to any number of people at any one time: 'We continually shed our constituent atoms into the world and acquire new ones in the process. Some of these elements eventually find their way in the bodies of other human beings. Parts of Alexander the Great, Edgar Allan Poe, and every other person you could name quite literally live on within us at this moment. How is God, in all His goodness and ingenuity, going to sort this out?' It makes the Sadducees' question to Jesus in Matt. 22:23–28 seem tame by comparison.

11. Go on, I dare you: find a Christian group somewhere to prove me wrong. The Internet is a wonderful thing.

12. Peter L. Berger, *A Rumor of Angels: Modern Society and the Rediscovery of the Supernatural*, 1st edn (Garden City, NY: Doubleday, 1969), pp. 49–75, esp. 52ff.

function of Paul's argument, even if the details of the argument don't work for us today.

In short: identify the objections in Paul's day, and use them to pinpoint similar objections – and different objections – in our own. Then make use of Paul's arguments to answer them.

Summary: *Refutatio*

Refutatio was intended to . . .
- Counter opponents' arguments directly;
- Portray opponents' characters and motives in a bad light;
- Anticipate objections and counter-arguments;
- Answer criticism.

When preaching *refutatio* . . .
- Understand that the objections may be hypothetical;
- Look for similar objections in our own day and answer them using the text;
- Employ the principle itself, anticipating objections that may arise in our own context.

Exercise

Read Romans 6.

- What are the objections (real or anticipated) that Paul addresses?
- How might similar objections be raised in our own day?
- What different objections might be raised?
- How might we use the text to answer these objections in our sermon?

8. *PERORATIO*

In conclusion, then . . .
So, to sum up . . .
Finally, brothers and sisters . . .

Let's be honest: when we utter those words as preachers, it's usually
a signal that we want our longsuffering congregation to hang in there
and pay attention for just a few minutes longer as we make one last
effort to be as concise and practical as we should have been in the
first place. For said congregation, it's usually a signal to pack away
their Bibles and start thinking about what's for lunch. A powerful
closing is difficult to master.

This is probably because a conclusion is trying to do a number
of things at once – a good recipe for confusion. At the end of a
sermon, we're trying to remind people of content they've already
heard – packaged in a concise, memorable way – while still holding
their interest. In addition, we're trying to inspire them not merely to
remember the content, but to *act on it* in a concrete way. And integral
to *that* is an appeal not just to their intellect but to their deeper desires

and emotions. It's often the most complicated part of a sermon and the most difficult to get 'right'.

The ancient rhetorical handbooks called this concluding part of the speech the *peroratio*, and spoke of three functions. (I've put the Latin terms in for the sake of completeness, but you don't need to worry about remembering them.)

Enumeratio (or *recapitulatio*) was the practice of summing up the main points of the speech. It was designed to help the audience remember them, as well as to show the cumulative effect: *Look at all these arguments I've presented – I must be right!*

Indignatio was where the speaker tried to arouse in the audience strong emotions about the subject in order to sway them to his case – we'll look at this more closely in chapter 10 when we talk about *pathos*.

Conquestio (or *commiseratio*) was an appeal for sympathy for the speaker or his cause. This is connected with *ethos* argument relating to the character of the speaker, which is the subject of chapter 9.

In essence, the *peroratio* functioned as an emotive summing-up. We see each of these aspects in the *peroratio* of Galatians:

> [12]Those who want to impress people by means of the flesh are trying to compel you to be circumcised. The only reason they do this is to avoid being persecuted for the cross of Christ. [13]Not even those who are circumcised keep the law, yet they want you to be circumcised that they may boast about your circumcision in the flesh. [14]May I never boast except in the cross of our Lord Jesus Christ, through which the world has been crucified to me, and I to the world. [15]Neither circumcision nor uncircumcision means anything; what counts is the new creation. [16]Peace and mercy to all who follow this rule – to the Israel of God. [17]From now on, let no one cause me trouble, for I bear on my body the marks of Jesus. (Gal. 6:12–17)

The whole section functions as an *enumeratio*, recapping the key arguments of the epistle. The *indignatio* of verses 12–13 arouses the stronger emotions against the self-serving Judaizers. And the final *conquestio* in verse 17 seeks sympathy for Paul's cause, since he has bravely suffered for the sake of Christ – the very thing the Judaizers are trying to avoid.[1] This concluding emotional appeal was written in Paul's own handwriting (6:11), heightening the *pathos*.

If the function of the *peroratio* was to be emotive and memorable, the style certainly matched: it was short and sharp, with fewer connecting words and lots of commands and exhortations. It sent the message: *Now that I've proven my case, do this in response!*

Some of Paul's briefer *peroratio* sections highlight this, with very short phrases and sentences (far shorter, for example, than the sentences in Paul's opening thanksgivings!). Here, I've altered the NIV's word order and punctuation to reflect the effect in Greek more closely:

> *1 Corinthians 16:13–14*
>> Be on your guard! Stand firm in the faith!
>> Be courageous! Be strong!
>> Do everything in love.

> *1 Thessalonians 5:16–22*
>> Rejoice always. Continually pray.
>> In everything give thanks – for this is God's will
>>> for you in Christ Jesus.
>> The Spirit, do not quench.
>> Prophecies, do not despise – but test them all.
>> The good, hold firmly; but from every kind of evil,
>>> hold back.

As you can see (or hear, if you read these out loud), as well as being short and sharp, the phrasing is more poetic and powerful.

---

1. See Hans Dieter Betz, 'Literary Composition and Function of Paul's Letter to the Galatians', *New Testament Studies* 21 (1975), p. 357; this analysis is also adopted by Ben Witherington III, *Grace in Galatia: A Commentary on St Paul's Letter to the Galatians* (Grand Rapids: Eerdmans, 1998), p. 444.

Summary: The three functions of the *peroratio*

Enumeratio/recapitulatio	Sum up the main points of the speech. To help memory and heighten the cumulative effect.
Indignatio	Arouse the strong emotions (*pathos*) in the service of the speaker's case.
Conquestio/commiseratio	Appeal for sympathy for the speaker or his cause.

The *peroratio* was delivered in a short, sharp style full of commands and with few connecting words.

Preaching from a *peroratio*

We could describe the *peroratio*, then, as an emotive summing-up with a punchy, commanding style. But how does that help us preach on a *peroratio*?

A reminder

If the text we're preaching from contains an *enumeratio*, the sermon should have a similar function, bringing to mind the key points of the whole epistle. It could help the congregation remember the significant lessons of the series – and not just as a series of isolated ideas, but to show how they have been a unified argument for the truth of the *propositio*. It packages the series in our hearers' minds.

If there's no recap present in the text, we might need to provide one. After all, we probably dealt with the *propositio* and key arguments over several weeks – not in one sitting, as was the case with the original audience. So for the *peroratio* to function the way it did in the text, we might need to include 'the story so far'.

This is particularly important if we're going to use emotions to persuade, as was the function of the *peroratio*. An emotive sermon in isolation may come across as manipulative, but when the emotional appeal is made in the light of all the rational argument that comes before it, the appeal is functioning the way it did in the original text.

The emotions

Our passage may contain *indignatio*, arousing the stronger emotions in order to persuade. In chapter 10 we'll discuss in more detail the use of emotional appeals in preaching – and the danger of it crossing over into manipulation. For now, though, two observations will do.

First, the kind of expository model which simply says *tell them what the text says and let the Spirit apply and persuade* is clearly at odds with the way Paul and the other New Testament writers operated. This is particularly so in the *peroratio* sections. The scriptural model is to engage the heart as well as the head.

Second, if we're respecting the function of the text, a sermon on a *peroratio* will have a particularly passionate and emotive character – perhaps more so than other sermons in the series. If the text is becoming more urgent and emotive, our sermon should do likewise.

The passage may also contain *conquestio*, seeking sympathy for the speaker or the cause. We'll also deal with that in chapter 9 which is about *ethos*.

Style

A *peroratio* contained short, sharp phrases and a more commanding tone. So how do we reflect this in our preaching?

The first aspect of style – the brief, urgent phrases with few connecting words – sometimes makes a sermon on a *peroratio* difficult to unify. Rather than having a complete argument or paragraph on a particular topic, we might get only one phrase before moving on to the next (reread the *peroratio* from 1 Thessalonians to see what I mean). This means there will probably be more 'points' than in other sermons.

Despite these changes in topic, remember that they're all still unified by how they relate to the *propositio*, even if that unifying logic isn't explicit in the text. For example:

- The diverse commands in the *peroratio* of 1 Thessalonians are, essentially, different ways of continuing to 'live in order to please God' – the key exhortation in 4:1.
- The commands in the *peroratio* of 1 Corinthians (16:13, 'Be on your guard; stand firm in the faith; be courageous; be strong') can all be understood as calls to be watchful/resolute/ courageous in promoting unity and resisting factionalism, particularly in the light of the next verse ('Do everything in love') and the subsequent self-sacrificial example of Stephanas's household.

They're also likely to be reminders of topics or points from previous sermons in the series, so they don't need to be as fully worked.

The second aspect of style – the frequent use of commands and exhortations – can also help to create a sense of unity. Even if the subject matter changes rapidly, unity can be found in the very fact that they're all rapid-fire commands. Since the *peroratio* is the emotional call to action of the speech, then on one level the unifying principle is simply: *What should we do in response to all that we've heard?* God says (1) . . . , (2) . . . , (3) . . .

This final sermon in the series will, more so than the others, seek to spell out the 'so what?' of the entire epistle. It will be more application-heavy, since there isn't as much to exegete in a command – and the logical and theological foundations for that command were probably laid out in more detail earlier in the epistle and dealt with in earlier sermons. For this reason it will instruct more directly, telling our hearers what God would have them do, rather than spending time going through all the reasoning and weighing up the benefits (as the main body of the epistle did). It's now time to cut to the chase and *live it*.

Summary: Preaching from a *peroratio*

The sermon recaps the key ideas of the whole epistle.

The tone of the sermon matches the emotive nature of the text.

The style is more direct and application-heavy, dealing with the 'so what?' of the entire preaching series.

PART 3

TYPES OF PROOF

When it comes to important buying decisions – such as for cars, houses and insurance policies – we like to think we're rational beings; that we're persuaded by logic and sound argument. A lot of the time, however, we end up signing that insurance contract because we built up a rapport with the salesperson. Or we buy that car because of how it made us feel – and then rationalize our decision after the fact. Marketers know that we buy on the basis of rapport and desire just as much as through rational argument: in fact, truth be told, usually *more* than through rational argument.

The ancient handbooks on how to write speeches knew this, too. Aristotle famously divided the arguments (or 'proofs') used in speeches into three kinds: 'The first depends upon the moral character of the speaker, the second upon putting the hearer into a certain frame of mind, the third upon the speech itself, in so far as it proves or seems to prove.'[1]

---

1. *Rhetoric*, 1.2.3.

We could call these three types of persuasive argument rapport, emotions and logic, respectively. Or, if we were ancient Greek speech-writers, *ethos, pathos* and *logos*.

Ethos, for Aristotle, was all about the trustworthy character of the speaker – providing reasons why we should trust his advice. At one point, he calls ethos 'the most effective means of proof',[2] especially in deliberative rhetoric. Later (in Cicero and Quintilian), the definition of ethos broadened to include any arguments that produced sympathy for the speaker or his case.

Pathos was about producing in the audience the stronger emotions, such as love, hatred, fear or pity, in order to influence their opinions. Aristotle sought to evoke pathos by giving rational reasons why the audience should feel a particular way. The later, Latin writers sought to do the same by their use of rhetorical techniques, such as exaggeration, amplification, striking imagery, and even the sounds and rhythms of the words themselves.

Logos was about demonstrating the rationality of the speaker's case, either deductively (proceeding from agreed premises and taking them to their logical conclusion) or inductively (citing examples and making analogies).

The next three chapters look at each of these types of proof – or modes of argument – and how we might preach from New Testament texts that operate in these different modes.

Note that the *probatio* section of the speech (*probatio* is Latin for 'proof') would mostly – but not exclusively – focus on logos arguments. The opening sections were the natural home for most of the ethos arguments, and the closing *peroratio* usually featured more pathos.

---

2. Ibid., 1.2.4.

9. PREACHING ETHOS

We're more likely to be persuaded by people we like, by people who are like us and by people who are on our side. Salespeople know this. They work hard at establishing rapport. They present themselves as likeable people, and try to find – or, sometimes, manufacture – little connections that make us see them as being 'just like us'. And above all, they want to come across as being *on your side*, with your interests at heart – going into battle with the 'evil sales manager' to get you the best deal they can.[1]

Ancient speech-writers were little different, seeing the *ethos* (character) of the speaker as integral to the task of persuasion. Sometimes, they said, it was the *most* important factor – especially when it came to subjects where there could be no certainty.[2] They wanted to come across as trustworthy voices who had their hearers'

1. Robert B. Cialdini, *Influence: The Psychology of Persuasion*, rev. edn (New York: HarperCollins, 2007), pp. 130–131, 140.
2. Aristotle, *Rhetoric*, 1.2.4. See also Cicero, *On Oratory*, 2.184, and Quintilian, *Institutes of Oratory*, 3.8.13.

interests at heart, not their own. They wanted their audience to feel
sympathy for them and their cause.

In fact, this was pretty much the first order of business in a
speech: establish rapport; build your ethos in the eyes of the
audience. For this reason, the opening parts of a speech tended to
contain the most ethos arguments. (Remember the function of the
exordium? To raise the topic and establish rapport.) This was done
regardless of how well your audience already knew you. Even if you
already had a good reputation, you were expected to remind them
why that was the case – to rehearse the evidence of your good
character and goodwill towards them. This is why sometimes Paul
can come across as a bit touchy and defensive to our ears. (*No, I am
an apostle,* really! *Let me spell out my credentials again, at length . . .*)
Speaking for twenty-first-century Australians, we're trained from
birth not to blow our own trumpets. More than that, if someone
tries to blow our trumpet *for* us, we instinctively put our hand inside
the bell to muffle the sound, so to speak. And those who *do* dare to
blow their own trumpets won't be establishing much ethos any time
soon. In the first-century world, though, such brassiness was
common. It was expected. *Remind me again why I should listen to you
and take your advice.*

The important thing to remember is that ethos-building wasn't
supposed to be an end in itself. (Unfortunately, that's kind of what
happened with a particular flavour of rhetoric, dubbed 'sophistic'.
It became more about impressing the audience with your rhetorical
skill than about the subject at hand. We'll see Paul combat this abuse
of rhetoric later, in 1 Corinthians.) The establishing of the speaker's
ethos was for the purpose of persuasion: winning the audience over
to the speaker's case. It had a function in the light of the *propositio*.

The purpose of ethos in the epistles

So when New Testament writers use an ethos argument, the first
question we need to ask is: To what end? Or more concretely: How
does it support the central *propositio* of the text? Only then can we
understand its function in the letter, and from that get an idea of
how the sermon should function in our own setting. That is, we

work out the *intended effect* of the ethos argument in the text in order to produce an *analogous effect* in our own setting.[3] So before we discuss how to preach ethos, let's look at a few examples of ethos-building in the New Testament to see how they function.

In Galatians we see an *exordium* (1:6–10) and long *narratio* (1:11 – 2:14), which are all about Paul's ethos. Right from the opening address he says that his authority as an apostle comes from God, not human beings (1:1). In the *narratio*, Paul tells the story of how he was commissioned directly by God, independently of the Jerusalem leadership (1:11–24). This ethos claim is important, as in the letter Paul is going to confront the Jerusalem leadership and implicitly claim to be speaking for God. Then he points out that – for what it's worth – the Jerusalem 'pillars' *did* previously endorse his apostleship to the Gentiles (2:9). By this, Paul suggests that *they* are the ones who are now being inconsistent, and possibly even hypocritical, so he builds his own ethos at the expense of theirs.

To back this up, Paul then tells what happened previously in Antioch (2:11–14). Peter, in a moment of weakness, withdrew from eating with Gentiles because he was afraid of what *people* (the Judaizers) might say. By contrast, Paul – who wasn't a people-pleaser, as he's already claimed in the *exordium* (1:10) – stood up to Peter and the Judaizers, publicly rebuking them for their hypocrisy. (The summary of the speech he gave in Antioch then becomes the *propositio* of the Galatian letter.) Thus Paul emerges from the story with his ethos enhanced. He's the only one who's remained true to his convictions – unlike Peter, Barnabas and the others. If he's about to admonish the Galatians for being 'bewitched' by the Judaizers (3:1) into departing from the truth, it does his argument no harm to show how he himself resisted such pressure. *I'm the one you can trust in this situation. God's on my side, and I've consistently stood*

---

3. I say 'analogous' because in many cases producing the *same* effect is either impossible or pointless. We're not part of the original situation involving, say, Paul and one of his churches, so it can't be identical. But the effect we produce in our sermon still needs to have strong points of contact with the original, if we're preaching the true rhetorical intent of the text.

up for the truth! Paul's ethos claims (divine commission, consistent conduct, and boldness in the face of opposition) directly support the central argument of Galatians.

In Romans, Paul's in a different mode. Unlike in Galatians, he doesn't know the church personally, so he doesn't have the same authority. Nor is there a crisis needing urgent correction. Here he writes as an outsider, seeking to build ethos for the first time in order to gain a hearing. He does this by:

- Complimenting them, acknowledging their reputation (1:8);
- Invoking God as witness to how much he prays for them (1:9);
- Expressing his desire to see them, and softly countering anyone who might ask 'What's taken you so long?' by attributing it to external forces and God's plan (1:10, 13);
- Describing his motivation as wanting to impart to them a 'spiritual gift' (1:11), but not in a way that makes him sound superior (1:12).

The intention is that by this point the believers in Rome will be positively disposed to hear Paul – *he likes us and he has our interests at heart* – as he begins his *propositio* (1:16–17).

As we saw in chapter 3, 1 Thessalonians is epideictic, praising the already held values of the Thessalonian believers. Paul's ethos strategy during the first three chapters is twofold. First, he compliments his audience for their reputation, and for how quickly they turned from idols to embrace the gospel (1:4–10). Second, he reminds them of how he has their best interests at heart: he came with pure motives – not seeking praise from people, not seeking financial gain – treating them as a loving father would (2:1–16), and desperately longing to see them again (2:17 – 3:13). The point of all this is to strengthen their connection to Paul. After all, he was only there for three weeks before he got chased out of town! And he does all this so that they might hear and respond to his exhortation: to continue living faithfully to God all the more (4:1).

In a similar way, 1 John is an epideictic sermon addressed to a church after a devastating split. It seeks to rebuild the audience's own ethos, reminding them that the evidence of their character is obedience to God and loving one another (5:2). At the same time it seeks to diminish the ethos of those who left, describing them as liars (2:22) and antichrists (2:18) who lead others astray (2:26) – they are outsiders who, by leaving, show that they never truly belonged (2:19; 4:5–6). In 1 John, ethos arguments are vital to accomplishing its central purpose: encouraging the faithful to persevere and remain within the group.

We could also point to the extended defence of Paul's actions in 2 Corinthians, rebuilding his ethos in the eyes of a church that had become estranged from him; or the ethos of citizen-Paul-in-chains writing to the Philippian church so that they, too, might follow his example and be faithful, bold citizens of the heavenly empire – but I think you get the idea of how ethos arguments work. (Later, we'll also look at an example sermon on 1 Corinthians 1, where questions over Paul's ethos are tied up with the factionalism that's the subject of the *propositio*.)

Right now, we need to get to the issue of how we *preach* ethos-based texts today. To do that, we need to stop for a bit and ask a crucial question: *Whose ethos?*

Whose ethos?

Whose ethos should we be seeking to establish when preaching on ethos texts? If we look at what the texts are doing, most of the time it's about the author's ethos – which makes perfect sense in the original context. But how does that translate to a contemporary sermon? Occasionally it's God's ethos, on whose behalf the human author is speaking. How does that work with ancient speech conventions? And sometimes (as is the case in 1 Corinthians 1), both are intertwined. Moreover, in a sermon we add a third layer to all of this: the ethos of the preacher. How does all this fit together? Let's look at these one at a time.

The divine ethos

The most straightforward is the divine ethos: the character and trustworthiness of God. It's straightforward for a couple of reasons.

First, it's not unusual for an ancient orator to be speaking on behalf of another. Originally, people were supposed to speak for themselves in court or when publicly attacked in the political sphere, but not everyone could do it well. They started to employ speech-writers to write the speeches for them, which they'd then memorize and deliver. This soon evolved into the speech-writers' *delivering* the speeches on their behalf. And so the practice of attorneys speaking for their clients began (eventually charging for it in six-minute increments). In these scenarios, say the handbooks, the ethos of *both* the speaker and the client is important.[4] So Paul can promote both his own ethos and the ethos of the one on whose behalf he speaks.

Second, the divine ethos is the one constant in the two settings: the original setting of the text and the contemporary setting of our sermon. God's character and trustworthiness are clearly still relevant to our audience today, more so than the human author of the biblical text (the human author's ethos isn't irrelevant, but he is no longer an active player in the rhetorical situation).

However, there's one small difference we need to be aware of: the ethos-building strategy of the text *may not* produce the same effect on our audience as it did on the original audience. The logic of the argument may be based on cultural assumptions or social situations that our hearers no longer naturally share. Alternatively, the imagery may be so foreign that it needs recasting in order to be effective today. To achieve the same effect we may need to preach it differently.

One example of this might be the frequent use of Old Testament stories and imagery as evidence of God's faithful character. This will still *make sense* to our hearers, but depending on their biblical literacy – or how strongly they identify with being the 'faithful remnant' of Israel – it may not have as powerful an emotional effect. (This is even more the case when preaching to non-believers who are unlikely to see the Hebrew Scriptures as authoritative.) For this reason, without neglecting the Old Testament stories and images used by the New Testament writers, we might achieve a similar effect in our sermons by also rehearsing the accounts of God's faithfulness in our own shared story as a congregation. Similarly, where the

---

4. Cicero, *On Oratory*, 2.182.

New Testament frequently steals imagery from first-century culture (such as the Roman emperor, who was worshipped as a saviour-benefactor) and uses it for Christ,[5] we may need to recast some of it to be effective.

Given the uniqueness of each preaching context, the ways in which different preachers do this will vary greatly. The process, however, can be informed by asking the following four questions about the biblical text and our preaching context:

1. What about the divine ethos is being communicated in the biblical text?
2. What effect was that intended to produce in the original audience?
3. What are some of the 'blocks' which will prevent our audience from experiencing that same effect?[6]
4. In the light of this, what might our sermon do in order to produce that same effect?

The ethos of the New Testament author

As well as seeking to build God's ethos, the New Testament texts will sometimes build the ethos of the biblical author. This is where it can get messy. We've seen a number of examples in this chapter where Paul – at length – defends his own ethos. And not just in a general 'if anyone happened to be wondering if I'm a real apostle, let me spend a few moments putting that one to rest' kind of way,

---

5. See e.g. 'saviour' in Phil. 3:20; 'saviour' along with two words associated with benefactor-praise, 'goodness and lovingkindness', in Titus 3:4–5 (literal translations); and the benefits of 'citizenship' and 'peace' being ascribed to Christ, not the emperor, in Eph. 2:11–14. Further, see Frederick W. Danker, *Benefactor: Epigraphic Study of a Graeco-Roman and New Testament Semantic Field* (St Louis: Clayton, 1982), p. 330.

6. David Buttrick talks about congregational 'blocks' in receiving and obeying the message of the text (David Buttrick, *Homiletic: Moves and Structures* [Philadelphia: Fortress, 1987], p. 47). I'm applying this idea here to the process not just of understanding and obeying, but also of *experiencing* the full rhetorical effect of the text.

but often in a very situation-specific way, because his ethos is *a part of the problem he's addressing.* Whether it be his right to chastise the Galatians, or his right to give up his right to earn a living from the gospel in Corinth, Paul's ethos can't be bracketed from the rhetorical situation. Which leads to the question: What's Paul's ethos got to do with *us* in the twenty-first century?

A lot of the time, the answer is 'not much' – at least, not directly. For most of our hearers, Paul's status as an apostle who speaks for God is not in doubt. And even for those who might question Paul's apostolic authority, the reasons why they do so are unlikely to be his (allegedly) unimpressive public-speaking skills (1 Cor. 1:17), his refusal to accept financial support from some churches (1 Cor. 9:3–4, 15) or his progressive stance on food laws and circumcision (Gal. 2:14). So what do we do with these kinds of texts, when their original function seems no longer relevant?

Back in chapter 5, we looked at how various commentators have applied the *narratio* of Galatians. The tendency has been to draw object lessons from elements of the narrative or to use the text to explore our own secondary questions – such as the nature of a person's conversion or call to ministry; but is this approach faithful to our conviction that the function of our sermon should be driven by the rhetorical function of the text? Commenting on Galatians 1 – 2, Scot McKnight offers this word of caution:

> In order to apply this biography of Paul we must first discern its essential purpose – and if that purpose is Paul's independence from Jerusalem and his direct revelation from Jesus Christ, then his biography is not as directly relevant [to us] as we might have initially thought. In fact, we should admit that we frequently apply secondary meanings of a text rather than its primary meaning.[7]

However, McKnight then gives some mixed messages. Without much in the way of justification, he goes on to allow for 'secondary

---

7. Scot McKnight, *Galatians: From Biblical Text . . . to Contemporary Life*, NIV Application Commentary (Grand Rapids: Zondervan, 1995), p. 74.

application' which is *not* derived from the original function of the text. He then gives far more space in his commentary to some of these 'secondary' issues – while strongly maintaining that they *are* secondary. It seems that in the absence of a clearly relevant primary application, his (commendable) desire to apply *all* of Scripture has led to a focus on applications which are, at best, tangential. And – lest I appear uncharitable to McKnight, of whom I'm a big fan – this is not uncommon.

I don't think the problem is simply to do with awareness of the role of ethos in ancient rhetoric and how it functioned in the original rhetorical situation (although this is an important first step); I think that we need a *model* for applying ethos arguments in a contemporary setting. So here is one such model: three ways in which the ethos of a New Testament author might legitimately be of significance for us today.

Biblical authority

The most obvious way the biblical author's ethos relates to us is to do with authority. This is utterly consistent with the original function of the text, in which the authors establish their ethos so that their God-given authority is recognized when they speak. For example, the ethos arguments in Galatians – from Paul's account of his commissioning by the risen Christ, to his explanation of how he acted in line with his core gospel convictions – all contribute to establishing Paul's authority to speak on behalf of God. Although Paul is no longer with us in person, he speaks in the same way to us. Commissioned by God, writing Scripture inspired *by* God, his words are authoritative for us, too.

The specific arguments, however, might not be quite as relevant to us. Let's face it, do we really care what the Jerusalem 'pillars' thought (Gal. 2)? Is our culture really going to look down on Paul for having been a bi-vocational pastor who refused financial support (1 Cor. 9)? Yet the general principle remains: Paul's authority as an apostle came from God himself (Gal. 1:11–12; 1 Cor. 9:1), backed up by his conduct being consistent with his message (Gal. 2:14; 1 Cor. 9:18).

So far, so obvious: the New Testament authors speak to us with God's authority. Is there anything else?

A model to imitate

The second way we can apply ethos texts is as a model: the New
Testament author's character and conduct function as an example
for us to imitate. This is drawn from the universal conviction in the
ancient world that a teacher's words had to be matched by his
character and deeds, which were to be worthy of emulation.[8] And,
of course, there's Paul's explicit call to imitate him in his own
imitation of Christ (1 Cor. 11:1; we also see this idea in 1 Cor. 4:16;
Phil. 3:17; 2 Thess. 3:7–9). He also instructs Timothy and Titus to
be such an example for their own congregations (1 Tim. 4:12; Titus
2:7). Further, the writer to the Hebrews insists that his audience
imitate their leaders (Heb. 13:7).

To what extent are we to imitate the authors of the New
Testament? Clearly, this doesn't mean re-enact everything they did!
Does it, though, mean that everything that has been recorded in
Scripture should function as a prescriptive model for us? I don't
think so. At its most basic level, their character and conduct in
general can be an inspiring model that informs how we might
grow in Christlikeness, engage in ministry and so on; but I think
it functions as *primary application* only when it's part of the rhetorical function of the text. That is, we draw application from the
aspects of character or conduct being displayed which are pertinent
to the issue at hand. A particular action or attitude may well
be admirable and inspiring, but unless it's mentioned in order to
build ethos *in this particular rhetorical context*, it isn't primary
application.

For example, Paul's story in Galatians isn't intended to be a prescriptive model for how someone is called into ministry (i.e. wait
for a vision of the risen Jesus), or for the duration of ministry
training (three years) – or even for the necessity of ministry training
(it may well be a good idea, but the function of *this text* is not
to act as a paradigm for ministry training, as some have taken it

---

8. William S. Kurz, 'Narrative Models for Imitation in Luke–Acts',
   in Abraham J. Malherbe et al. (eds.), *Greeks, Romans, and Christians:
   Essays in Honor of Abraham J. Malherbe* (Minneapolis: Fortress, 1990),
   p. 171.

to be[9]). These biographical details are particular to Paul and they have a function within the rhetoric of the *narratio* – they support the assertion that Paul's commission came directly from God and independently of the Jerusalem church. At no point is he relating these details in order for others entering ministry to emulate him.

By contrast, Paul's conduct *is* a model for us when he seeks the approval of God rather than people (Gal. 1:10), opposes the 'false believers' (2:4–5) and confronts a reputable leader like Peter when he's wrong (2:11–14). Why is this different? Because Paul narrates this conduct as the basis for establishing his ethos in this context. The problem is that some people are fearing people more than God, tolerating those who are adding to the gospel and not confronting leaders when they're wrong. Here, Paul models the kind of behaviour required whenever gospel truth is at stake. The rhetorical function is one of both establishing authority ('*listen to me* as I'm the one in this whole situation who's acting consistently with the gospel!') and inspiring emulation ('*imitate me* in resisting hypocrisy and false teaching').

To sum up: whenever New Testament authors are building their own ethos, they give us a model of character and conduct to imitate, insofar as these aspects of character and conduct relate to the context of their argument.[10]

Ethos in our own context
There is a third way we can apply ethos arguments to our own situation. It's less straightforward, but I think it's even more in tune

---

9. See Michael J. Anthony and James Riley Estep, eds., *Management Essentials for Christian Ministries* (Nashville: B&H, 2005), pp. 23–24; Dana Mathewson, *Call 2 Ministry: Exploring the Myths, the Mystery, and the Meaning of Following God's Call into Vocational Ministry* (Maitland, FL: Xulon, 2003), p. 85; Alvin Low, *Descending Into Greatness: Biblical Leadership* (Morrisville, NC: Lulu, 2006), pp. 14–16.

10. Tim MacBride, *Preaching the New Testament as Rhetoric: The Promise of Rhetorical Criticism for Expository Preaching*, Australian College of Theology Monograph Series (Eugene: Wipf & Stock, 2014), p. 149.

with the original intent. It's where we look at the whole rhetorical
context and work out how ethos is being used, so we can work out
how to use it in our own setting. Again, there's a series of questions
to help us do this:

1. What is the issue being addressed?
2. How does the New Testament writer use ethos to help
   address the issue?
3. Is there an analogous issue in our contemporary world?
4. How might ethos be similarly used to address our own
   issue? Or, to put it another way, if Paul, for example, were
   writing to our present situation, whose ethos would *he* be
   building?

Let's work that through with Galatians:

1. In simple terms, the issue is that the Judaizers were adding
   the boundary markers of Judaism (the food laws and
   circumcision) to Gentile converts, making it a 'different
   gospel' (1:6).
2. As we've seen, Paul builds his own ethos for two reasons:
   to re-establish his authority so he can rebuke the
   Judaizers and correct the Galatian believers; and to
   show that his character and conduct are in keeping with
   his convictions.
3. Are there any analogous issues in the contemporary church?
   Of course! This issue arises whenever a cultural practice or
   observance becomes a requirement – either for salvation or,
   more commonly, for acceptance as a member of a believing
   community.
4. Contemporary preachers can use both strands to Paul's
   ethos argument in speaking into such situations, citing Paul's
   authority to condemn such legalism, along with his example
   of how to resist it. These correspond to the first two ways of
   applying ethos arguments.

However, to stop there misses much of the persuasive effect of
the original ethos argument. Why? Because Paul was a participant

in the original situation, whereas today he speaks from afar. His example is one of historical precedent, rather than being an integral part of our situation. Pushing further, then, we might also ask: *Whose ethos would Paul seek to build today?* Or, to put it another way, who embodies the same ethos as Paul in condemning legalism and the imposition of cultural markers, and in standing up for gospel truth? We might mention specific individuals, where it's appropriate to do so; or, more generically, particular attitudes and actions that are in line with Paul's own example.

In my teens, I belonged to a conservative suburban church that had taken quite a gamble. It had been a dwindling congregation of older believers with a heart to do whatever it took to reach younger people. So they called as their new pastor someone who had only a few years back come to faith from a drug-taking hippie lifestyle. Pretty soon, the church was thriving again, reaching people from all kinds of backgrounds. One of the leading elders was quite traditional, sometimes butting heads with the new pastor – and sometimes for good reason. (Early on they did a deal: the New International Version could replace the King James Version if the pastor wore shoes.) Yet despite this elder's conservative upbringing – and occasionally, it seemed, against every fibre of his being – he embraced the radical changes that swept across the church. He'd happily stand each Sunday in his three-piece suit, shoulder to shoulder with a brand-new, barefoot Christian in torn board shorts, singing praises to God. And in doing so, he gave us a little glimpse of the great multitude from all backgrounds that will worship God in the age to come.

I've told this story many times, because his conduct embodies the biblical values which the situation called for. In a sense, I've been saying, 'Be imitators of him, as he is of Paul, as Paul is of Christ!' This is the kind of person whose ethos Paul would have built, I think, if he'd been in my church back in the 1980s.

Note that this persuasive strategy is different from simply providing reasons why we shouldn't add to the gospel. That would be a *logos* argument, and Paul gives plenty of those from the *propositio* onwards. Here, we're building the ethos of people who embody this principle (as Paul did in Gal. 2), honouring their behaviour in a way that inspires emulation.[11] In this way, we're moving beyond the ethos of just the New Testament author (who is no longer a direct participant in our context) and looking for people – or kinds of people – in our own context whose ethos embodies the message of the text.

The ethos of the preacher

There is a 'third ethos' in play in all this, of course. It's our own, as preachers. This isn't in the biblical text, which is why I'm not going to spend much time on it (my focus here is on bringing the rhetoric of the text into the present). However, it *is* just as important, and I think it connects with the ethos in the text that we've been discussing in two ways. And they're both quite obvious and fundamental.

The first way relates to our authority to speak 'for God'. Although we're not apostles in that same sense, our authority to speak for God comes from the apostolic text that's the subject of our sermon. We establish this kind of ethos when we make it clear that we're preaching what the text says: we show our audience where in the text our content can be found and (at least some of) the process by which we arrived at our application. Instead of just expecting our congregation to 'trust us', we build ethos by making the source of our authority clear and explicit.

The second way relates to our conduct among the people to whom we preach. As was the case with orators in the first century, *our* ethos is established when our walk matches the talk. This is true *in general* about our preaching ministry, but it's also important in relation to the specific texts on which we preach. When we show, in an honest way, how *we* are trying to apply the text we're preaching on – or are struggling to apply it – our ethos functions in a similar way to the ethos of the biblical author.

---

11. We could do similarly with the ethos arguments found in the first four chapters of 1 Corinthians, building the ethos of those who embrace substance over style, and godly 'weakness' over human sophistication (see the example sermon at the end of this chapter). Or think back to the example *narratio* sermon on Phil. 1:12–30 in which we noted not just Paul's ethos, but the ethos of all who joyfully suffer for the gospel.

Summary: Preaching ethos

The divine ethos . . .

- is still relevant, but may need to be communicated differently.

The ethos of the New Testament author . . .

- relates to biblical authority;
- functions as a model for imitation;
- prompts us to ask: Whose ethos would be built *in our own setting*?

The ethos of the preacher . . .

- relates to the authority of the preacher;
- should function as a model for imitation.

Exercise

Read Philippians 2:19–30, in which Paul builds the ethos of Timothy and Epaphroditus, providing them as examples of the kind of conduct appropriate to a good citizen of heaven: selfless, even to the point of risking death.

Whose ethos would *you* build in order for your sermon to have a similar function?

Ethos strategies

Once we've worked out whose ethos is being established by the text – and therefore whose ethos our sermon ought to establish – we can look at the wider question of 'how'. What follows is a very brief outline of the kinds of strategies used both by first-century orators and by the New Testament authors to build ethos. This is important, as we need to be able to identify these strategies if we're going to use them (or something like them) in our own setting.

Trustworthiness and character
The most straightforward way of establishing ethos was to display good sense, goodness and goodwill. According to Aristotle, all three are essential. Without good sense, your opinions can't be trusted;

without goodness, your morals can't be trusted; and without goodwill, your intentions towards your audience can't be trusted.[12]

We could find plenty of examples of this throughout the New Testament, but for now we'll just take a few from 2 Corinthians, in which Paul is in the position of having to *defend* his ethos. There, he defends the logic behind his change of plans (1:15–18), testifying to his good sense. He asserts his goodness by describing his 'integrity and godly sincerity' (1:12) and that he takes 'pains to do what is right' in the eyes of God and other people (8:21). Paul makes a lot of the third aspect of trustworthiness – goodwill – claiming that his actions are for their benefit, not his (1:6, 23; 2:10; 7:2; 12:19), and contrasting his own ministry with that of those who are in it only for their own gain (2:17 – 3:3). Tellingly, he describes his audience as being his 'letter of recommendation', which was an ancient letter-type that attested to the ethos of its subject.

Narrating the facts
Another way of building ethos is in the way in which the facts of the matter are narrated. I dealt with this in chapter 5, when looking at the *narratio*.

Showing restraint
As I mentioned earlier in the chapter, building your own ethos isn't culturally appropriate in many Western societies, and certainly not in twenty-first-century Australian society. Although this wasn't the case in the Graeco-Roman world, there was still a point at which too much boasting could have a negative effect on the audience. Cicero suggested that speakers get around this 'by seeming to act against your inclination, because you are forced to do so'.[13]

We see Paul doing this numerous times in his mocking display of sophistic rhetoric in 2 Corinthians 11 – 13. He needs to make the point that he *can* match it with the 'super-apostles' in his speaking style if he so chooses, while not wanting to look as if he's joining in with their boasting. So he does it seemingly against his will, asking

---

12. Aristotle, *Rhetoric*, 2.1.5.
13. Cicero, *On Oratory*, 2.182.

his audience to bear with him 'in a little foolishness', breaking off mid-sentence to say he's speaking as a 'fool' and as someone 'out of my mind' (11:21, 23), and claiming that they had 'forced' him to boast in this way (12:11).

Negative ethos

Another way of building your own ethos was to discredit the ethos of your opponents.[14] (In the ancient world, honour was thought to be in limited supply; you could *gain* honour by taking honour from someone else.[15]) This was usually done by describing them using harsh, negative words, depicting their motives as self-serving and their conduct as shameful.

We don't need to look too hard to find New Testament examples of this, ranging from Jesus' critique of the Pharisees (Matt. 23) and Stephen's speech condemning Israel for consistently rejecting God's messengers (Acts 7), to John's portrayal of the 'antichrists' who left his church (1 John 2:18–28) and the 'depraved' false teachers in 2 Peter 2. In Galatians, Paul is scathing towards the Judaizers – they are 'perverting the gospel' (1:7) for their own interests (4:17; 6:13) and avoiding persecution through cowardice (6:12) – calling down a curse on them (1:8), and goading them to take their insistence on circumcision significantly further (5:12)! We see a similar portrayal of his opponents in Philippians (3:2, 19) and in the pastoral epistles (e.g. 1 Tim. 1:3–7; 4:1–2; 6:3–5; Titus 3:9–11).

The difficulty with these types of passages is that they don't translate well into contemporary Western culture. It was considered good form in the Graeco-Roman world to paint your opponents negatively, attacking their character just as much as their arguments. Today, though, the opposite is generally true in civilized debate (politics being the notable exception). This difference in cultural values means that if we simply replicate the rhetorical strategies of the New Testament, they will *function* quite differently – probably not commending our position to our hearers, but alienating them.

---

14. For example, see Cicero, *On Invention*, 1.16.

15. Jerome H. Neyrey, *Honor and Shame in the Gospel of Matthew*, 1st edn (Louisville: Westminster John Knox Press, 1998), pp. 17–18.

Scot McKnight, writing on Paul's depiction of his opponents in Galatians 1, makes this point very clear:

> But how do we talk about such perversions? Do we use the same kind of harsh rhetoric that Paul used? Again, our culture is different from Paul's. What was seen as an acceptable form of disagreement then may not be seen as acceptable today . . . The ancient world simply loved inflammatory language for expressing its differences. I can document a great deal of such language in their literature, but I have not been able to document any who thought such language was personally biased and out of line. The ancients delighted in overstatement, and overstatements were effectively countered with similar overstatements . . . Ours is not the ancient world. For this reason alone I believe we need to state our decisions more carefully and in a less inflammatory manner than Paul did in Galatians 1. What we need today is less tirade, less emotional outburst, and much more carefully constructed arguments that vindicate the truthfulness of the gospel of Jesus Christ.[16]

In sum, we need to communicate the passion and significance of such inflammatory rhetoric in the New Testament, while using the appropriate language of passionate-yet-measured debate that's considered persuasive and honourable in our own culture.

Matching the audience's ethos

Unlike the previous strategy, this next one is most assuredly *not* out of place today. It's the principle of matching your ethos to that of your audience, which Aristotle explains thus:

> Since everyone likes to hear speeches that are spoken in his own character [*ethos*], and speakers who resemble him, it is now easy to see what language we must employ so that both ourselves and our speeches may appear to be of such and such a character.[17]

Since people respond more favourably to those who resemble them, a persuasive speech will present the ethos of the speaker in

---

16. McKnight, *Galatians*, pp. 59–60.
17. Aristotle, *Rhetoric*, 2.13.16.

a way that matches the ethos of the audience. That is, speakers won't just present themselves as trustworthy; they'll present themselves as trustworthy *according to that audience's understanding of trustworthiness.*

We find this principle at work in both the rhetoric *and* the lifestyle of Paul, with his famous 'all things to all people' principle. And this has implications for our preaching.

First, it can help us understand the rhetorical purpose of an ethos text. It may tell us why Paul is building a *particular aspect of ethos* in the eyes of his audience. An obvious example is the way in which Paul builds ethos in Athens (Acts 17, showing his audience that he was well informed about pagan gods and Greek poets), which is quite different from his ethos-building strategy among Jewish believers (Acts 22; 26, in which he reminds his hearers of his former Pharisaic zeal in persecuting Christians).

Second, it challenges our own ethos. As Paul often matched his ethos to that of his audience, should we not do likewise? This is, of course, nothing new in the world of contextual evangelism. What we see here, though, is that being 'all things to all people' in our preaching is grounded both in Paul's own example specifically and in first-century rhetorical theory generally.

Third, it suggests an additional line of application for ethos texts in challenging our contemporary hearers. The very fact that Paul is adapting his own ethos to match that of his audience is an example of being all things to all people that is worthy of imitation. In other words, in applying ethos texts we don't just apply the ethos-building rhetorical strategy to our hearers; we also encourage our hearers to use that kind of ethos-building rhetorical strategy themselves. We urge them to follow Paul's example in being all things to all people as they present the gospel.

Summary: Ethos strategies

Demonstrating trustworthiness and character
Narrating the facts of the matter in a favourable light
Showing restraint when it comes to self-promotion
Portraying the ethos of opponents in a negative light
Displaying the aspects of ethos valued by the audience

(This corresponds with the second way in which the ethos of the New Testament author is relevant to us: as an example to be imitated.)

When ethos is subverted

As well as noticing when these (and other) ethos-building strategies are used by the New Testament authors, we should also take notice when standard ethos conventions are ignored or turned on their head: when ethos is subverted. This may be even more significant, as it highlights what is *distinctive* about the New Testament writers, as opposed to what is merely conventional.[18]

Here are two quick examples from Paul:

- The subversion of boasting: Paul 'boasts' of what God has done (Rom. 5:2–3; 15:17–18; 1 Cor. 1:31; Gal. 6:14); in the fruit produced by his converts (1 Cor. 15:31; 2 Cor. 1:14; 7:4; Phil. 2:16; 2 Thess. 1:4); or even, perversely, in his own weakness (2 Cor. 11:30; 12:9).
- The subversion of shame: redefining what is shameful in the eyes of society as being honourable in the eyes of God, whether it be suffering and imprisonment (Phil. 1:12; Col. 1:24; 2 Tim. 2:8, 12, 16), or even the claim not to be using eloquence or the 'wisdom of words' (1 Cor. 1:17; 2:1).

Once we've worked out that traditional ideas of ethos are being subverted by the New Testament, how does that impact our preaching? Here's another set of questions to help us work through it, which I've briefly answered in relation to 1 Corinthians 1 for illustration:

---

18. 'In the field of political, social and religious history differences are more important than similarities.' Arnaldo Momigliano, *On Pagans, Jews, and Christians*, 1st edn (Middletown, CT: Wesleyan University Press, 1987), p. 8.

1. What cultural view of ethos is Paul seeking to subvert?
   Status-seeking through public speaking (or being associated with a particular speaker), and judging status according to the world's values.
2. Why does he wish to subvert it? That is, what aspect of it is incompatible with the gospel?
   The gospel is about humility, not status-seeking, and about judging things by God's values.
3. How does he seek to subvert it?
   He doesn't play the game; he refuses to impress them with his speaking skills or other worldly status markers.
4. Are there views similar to (1) in our own culture?
   Of course! They may not be focused on public oratory, but the cult of celebrity is alive and well, as is status-through-association. More broadly, the world's way of judging status can easily be imported into the church, just as it was in Corinth.
5. Why might we wish to subvert them? That is, are they incompatible with the gospel?
   For the same reasons as Paul: we ought to judge by God's values, not the world's.
6. How might we subvert them, taking our cues (in the first instance) from Paul's strategy?
   The most obvious way is to avoid the cult of personality in our preaching ministry, but there are plenty of other ways in which churches uncritically adopt the way the world views status – there is much scope for application here.

Exercise

The sample ethos sermon, which appears next, fleshes out this process into a real-life sermon. First, though, have a think about it for yourself.

- How does Paul build Christ's ethos in Colossians 1:15–23?
- How does Paul build his own ethos in Colossians 1:24 – 2:5?
- How would you apply these two texts?

AN ETHOS SERMON

This sermon on 1 Corinthians 1:17 – 2:5 was first preached in 2009 and draws on the strategies outlined in chapter 9. Again, I've left it written 'for the ear'. Some of the situation-specific illustration and application has been omitted.

Some Christians seem to wear their faith almost as a fashion accessory. They've carefully crafted their 'brand' of Christianity as a fashion statement – a means of projecting their image to the world; a way of displaying their style, their sophistication or even their carefully crafted image of *not* appearing fashion-conscious.

> Begin with the problem in our world – the way we bring the world's status markers into the church.

For some of us, we can wear our knowledge of the Scriptures like a Scouting merit badge; the kinds of conferences we attend and the books we read become part of our identity. For others, our preference for cutting-edge café-fellowship over traditional churches gives us a smug sense of superiority. Or maybe we use our taste in Christian music to help define our personal 'brand' – the image we present to the world. Within the church, we mimic the status symbols of the world, giving them a Christian flavour.

As followers of Christ, have we taken up our cross only to turn it into bling?

> Transition to the analogous problem in the world of the text.

This is essentially what many of the Christians had done in Corinth two thousand years ago, with disastrous results for the unity of the church.

As we saw in the previous passage, they were divided around different leaders – or, more accurately, different *speakers*. 'I am of Paul,' some say. 'I am of Apollos,' cry others. Divided over *preachers*, for heaven's sake! What's going on? Are they *insane*?

An 'entertain me' culture

No. They were just doing what everyone else did in Greek and Roman society. Back then, people listened to public speakers – believe it or not – for *entertainment*! As a spectator sport. Rallying behind their favourite 'performers' with great zeal, and getting into heated debates with those who disagreed, sometimes involving physical violence with the other tribes. Hard to believe, I know, when you look at, say, soccer crowds today.

There was also a pretty vigorous debate about the *function* of public speaking. Some wanted it to be functional and serious, reflecting its origins in the law courts and city councils. It shouldn't become a circus spectacle. Others were content to be entertained by a grand display of verbal brilliance, speaking not for any real purpose other than to amuse, to please; or to display how good you were at speaking. They thought that this kind of showy eloquence was an indicator of wisdom, of superiority. In musical terms, it was a choice between the earthy simplicity of, say, Norah Jones or Leonard Cohen on the one hand, and the vocal gymnastics of Mariah Carey or Stevie Wonder on the other.[19]

Now this attitude, this division over style – it had found its way into the Corinthian church, and everyone had an opinion. Some of the travelling speakers, like Apollos, were more down the Mariah Carey line. Now, that's not to say Apollos lacked substance; simply that he was happy to present the gospel using his accomplished public speaking skills in all their glory. And some in Corinth responded very warmly to his style.

Unfortunately, this caused some division, as it was the *opposite* to Paul's strategy. In verse 17 Paul makes it clear that he doesn't want to use such eloquence. He doesn't want it to get in the way of the power inherent in the gospel itself. Have a listen:

---

19. No sermon illustrations are harder to universalize than those involving popular music. For the record, the original comparison was between Australian folk-rock artist Missy Higgins and pop diva Mariah Carey.

> For Christ did not send me to baptise, but to preach the gospel – not
> with wisdom and eloquence [literally: the wisdom of speech], lest the
> cross of Christ be emptied of its power. (1:17)

In other words, he doesn't want to present a façade of wisdom through a clever and entertaining use of words. He wants the *real* wisdom of God to remain sharply in focus.

Of course, this doesn't mean Paul refuses to speak with great skill. Throughout his letters we see that he uses all kinds of well-crafted strategies to *persuade* people of the truth of the gospel. What it does mean is that he won't pander to people in their desire for style over substance. He refuses to be side-tracked by entertainment when he's preaching the gospel – which meant he came across as 'unsophisticated'. So those who wanted to use their faith as a fashion statement wouldn't be caught dead wearing 'brand Paul'. He wouldn't pander to their pretensions.

Let me stop and ask: Do you see the similarities with our *own* culture?

How we value style over substance. How we sit back and wait to be entertained in all aspects of life. How we set up little rivalries between 'performers' and cheer on those who appeal to our own preferences. How we've got our finger permanently poised over the remote, ready to change channel the second our *own* buttons aren't being pressed.

> Apply the *details* of the rhetorical situation to your own situation, as closely as possible.

And do you see how we can often bring this attitude into the church? The way we respond to various preachers sometimes – we behave like we're in the studio audience for an episode of *So You Think You Can Preach*.[20] Score cards at the ready, we can't wait for the SMS voting to start. Just like the ancient Greeks, we're ready to judge the quality of the oratory. And if our local pastor's not up to scratch, we'll just download the podcast of someone more famous, more entertaining. (One of the questions

---

20. This sermon predates the reality competition of the same name which was launched by a church in Detroit in 2015. I was sadly prescient.

I've started to hear in my preaching class is this one: How do I *compete* with an iPod?)

Or we rally around a particular Christian author, theologian or conference. And we might do so for many good, theological reasons. But we *also* do it, sometimes subconsciously, because those particular speakers and authors and organizations press our buttons. Their humour, or their intellect, or their passion and zeal. We like their style; we 'get it'. And that's great! But then we can begin to wear this as a badge of honour; a symbol of our theological pedigree. Just as some of the Corinthians tried to display their sophistication by attaching themselves to Apollos.

Acting out the world's values in the church

In fact, that's the broader issue that's at stake here. It's not just about speaking style; that's merely a symptom. The problem was that the Corinthians were simply acting out the values of the world – *in the church!*

After all, Corinth was a relatively new city; not a lot of 'old money' in Corinth. And the recently wealthy, the self-made rich – they tended to be more anxious about status; anxious to prove how cultured they were. And one way to show off your sophistication was to host the most eloquent speakers in your home.

> Broaden the problem from the specific (division around speakers) to the general underlying issue.

So the sort of Corinthian Christians who appeared in the style section of their local newspapyri – they would have been falling all over themselves to host the likes of Apollos – leaving Paul to the Norah Jones fans. They were bringing the world's value system into the church, and the squabbles that went along with it. They were competing for status in the church the same way people competed for status in the world.

How many problems in churches today are caused by our uncritical adoption of the world's way of doing things? The world's way of judging things? Of defining status, success and worth?

Again, Paul refuses to play that game. He won't pander to their pretensions. This whole passage today is a response to this attitude. A defence of why Paul prefers to *appear* unsophisticated; why he won't play the world's game.

God doesn't pander to our pretensions (1:18–25)

> Paul's strategy is to link his own 'ethos problem' with God's ('I'm just copying how God operates') and then proceed to defend that. So do we.

Because it's not just Paul who refuses to pander to our pretensions. It's God, too. That's Paul's first point. The whole gospel message is designed by God to undercut human wisdom. So that to those outside of God's people, it seems foolish – even ridiculous.

For the message of the cross is foolishness to those who are perishing, but to us who are being saved it is the power of God. (1:18)

And it's not just in the New Testament where this happens: it's been God's style from the very beginning. When God chose an old guy with no kids to become the father of many nations and the means by which the world would be blessed. When God then rescued a bunch of slaves from Egypt and made them his special people. When he picked out a king to defend them – from the smallest tribe; the youngest son; a shepherd boy whose most notable skills were slinging a stone and strumming a lyre.

Throughout the Old Testament, we see God refusing to play to our expectations. God *does* move in ways which are not only mysterious, but sometimes appear downright *foolish*. Which leads Paul in the next verse to quote Isaiah:

For it is written:
'I will destroy the wisdom of the wise;
    the intelligence of the intelligent I will frustrate.'
(1:19)

God doesn't pander to our pretensions. When God acts to save us, he does it through the most unlikely of ways. A crucified messiah – I mean, how *ridiculous* is that? God himself dying on a cross! Can you imagine hearing *that* concept for the first time?

It certainly sent the Jews for a spin. They were expecting a military hero like David or Solomon to come in, raise up an army and defeat the Romans. Instead, they got a carpenter from Nazareth who somehow managed to get himself *killed* by the Romans. And on a cross – the most shameful of all deaths! Even the Old Testament weighs in on that – describing anyone hung on a tree as being 'cursed'.

So, clearly, God wasn't pandering to any *Jewish* pretensions when he came up with *that* rescue plan for the world! He didn't bother with market research in Judean shopping malls; he didn't run it past any focus groups of Pharisees. In fact, he seemed to be deliberately messing with them. As Paul says in verse 22, 'Jews demand signs' – but even Jesus himself refused to perform on demand. Instead, they were given the message of Christ crucified, which Paul says is 'a stumbling-block to Jews'.

But God wasn't any kinder to the Greeks either. (Here the term 'Greek' refers to 'civilized non-Jews' – the majority of Paul's audience in Corinth.) Read from verse 22:

> Jews demand signs and Greeks look for *wisdom*, but we preach Christ crucified: a stumbling-block to Jews and *foolishness* to Gentiles . . . (1:22–23)

Just as Jesus refused to give signs to unbelieving Jews, Paul won't use the façade of eloquence desired by the Greeks. He won't pander to their pretensions to wisdom; to sophistication; to culture. In place of lofty arguments and flashy speech, he tells of a guy who got nailed to a cross for their sin. And who came back from the dead to bring them life.

Members of the Greek intelligentsia, then, needed to give up their preoccupation with human 'wisdom' and cultured speech – if they wanted to be saved. They needed to embrace the foolishness of a crucified saviour.

The gospel is a great leveller. Sure, it withstands intellectual scrutiny, as Luke was at pains to point out when he wrote Acts. But unlike Greek philosophy, the gospel doesn't pander to intellectuals and cultural elitists. In the gospel, God works in a way that messes with human pride.

> For since in the wisdom of God the world through its wisdom did not know him, God was pleased through the foolishness of what was preached to save those who believe. (1:21)

Be careful, then, that *your* intellectual pretensions don't get in the way of responding to the gospel.

That they don't make you *distort* the gospel into something that fits better with your prejudices and preferences.

Isn't that what's happened to some parts of the church over the past couple of centuries? In the face of scientific advancement and human achievement, some aspects of the gospel became a bit of an embarrassment. The idea of miracles: who needs that kind of superstition these days, when we can explain everything with science and cure everything with medicine? Or angels and demons: aren't they just relics of an unenlightened time, ignorant of hallucinogenic drugs and mental illness?

> Apply the rhetorical situation: the ways in which our culture's intellectual pretensions can get in the way of responding to the gospel.

And what about this *resurrection* nonsense? Surely they don't mean a *literal* rising from the dead! It's more a symbol of hope; a myth from pre-modern times which describes the spiritual enlightenment which comes to each of us. And don't get us started on the meaning of the cross. Jesus didn't die to atone for our sin, to satisfy God's wrath, in an act of cosmic child abuse. He died as an *example* for us all, showing us how much God loves us . . .

Do you see how the intellectual pretensions of *our* era can make the message of the cross seem like foolishness? How they can become a stumbling block for us? If we're not careful, we can start to overlook, ignore or even change some parts of the gospel message, to try and make it fit in with human wisdom. But it won't work. Because God has deliberately made it that way.

Where is the wise person? Where is the teacher of the law? Where is the
philosopher of this age? Has not God made foolish the wisdom of the
world? (1:20)

If you're a scientist, or if you've studied the humanities, it's
often harder for you to come to Christ. Not because the gospel is
anti-scientific or doesn't make sense, but because it refuses to
play to the self-important assumptions of these disciplines: the
assumption that we humans have all the answers; that we humans
can solve all our own problems. The gospel says we can't. Only
God can. Only a God who – foolishly – died on a cross in our
place.

In the gospel, God does not pander to our pretensions. So that
alone should make us stop and think, whenever we catch ourselves
bringing our worldly pretensions into the church.

God prefers to work through the unpretentious (1:26–31)

But not only does God refuse to play our games; it seems he also
prefers to do his work through the *un*pretentious – through ordinary
people. People who aren't trying to pretend to be something better
than they are.

Throughout the Bible we see God's preference for the unpretentious. Again, think of David. Or the reluctant Moses. Or a prophet
like Amos, who may have spoken before kings, but was a simple
shepherd. Think of Jesus himself, and his unlikely origins. And what
about the leaders of the earliest church – a bunch of faithless,
clueless Galilean fishermen, through whom God somehow changed
the world! Most of the time, God prefers to work through the
unpretentious.

Which, in fact, described *most* of Paul's audience. When it came
down to it, most of the Corinthian Christians were *not* part of the
sophisticated latte-sipping set.

Brothers and sisters, think of what you were when you were called. Not
many of you were wise by human standards; not many were influential;
not many were of noble birth. (1:26)

They were poor and not highly educated. They were the ones who were being *excluded* by all the posturing over who could host the better speaker. So maybe they'd started to play the game, too – trying to increase their status by attaching themselves to the leaders of the Apollos faction, or the Peter faction, or even Paul's.

> Paul builds the ethos of the low-status majority (in a countercultural way), giving us a hint about whose ethos we might build today.

But Paul reminds them not to get caught up in all this.

The fact that they weren't important and sophisticated in the world's eyes makes them prime candidates in God's eyes: because God has chosen to work through people like *them*, in order to shame the self-important, the status-seekers.

> But God chose the foolish things of the world to shame the wise; God chose the weak things of the world to shame the strong. (1:27)

The gospel, then, is a great leveller. No-one can boast, because God is the source of all wisdom. And in his wisdom, he chose to use the most *un*likely vessels to carry out his plan.

> God chose the lowly things of this world and the despised things – and the things that are not – to nullify the things that are, so that no one may boast before him. (1:28–29)

Isn't that an encouragement?

After all, the vast majority of *us* are not important in the eyes of the world. We're not destitute, but most of us are *not* in the wealthiest 10% of Australian society. Most of us are *not* famous. Look around you! We're mostly *ordinary* people. Exactly the kind of people through whom God most often likes to work. And to work *extra*ordinary things.

> Imitate Paul's rhetorical strategy by building the ethos of the 'ordinary' people among your hearers.

This principle always reminds me of all the cross-cultural workers I know, whom I'm honoured to count as friends.

In one sense, they're all *ordinary* people. Sure, they've got particular gifts and abilities, as we all
have. But the one thing they're *not* is
pretentious. They're not flashy or
showy. They don't try to impress
people with their credentials. They
don't have a 'brand image' of themselves that they're constantly trying
to sell. I think that's *one* reason God
sent them to do the job they're doing.

> Build the ethos of the
> kinds of people Paul would
> point to today, if he were
> part of your situation –
> the kinds of people
> God often chooses to
> work through.

If you want God to use you, then
one of the qualifications seems to be a lack of pretension: where
our faith is about the glory of God among the nations, rather than
what kind of Christian image we'd like to project to the world. Don't
bring your worldly pretensions to church. Because most of the time,
God works through the *un*pretentious.

This is to show that salvation is by his power, not by human wisdom (2:1–5)

And God does this for a reason – which is also *Paul's* reason for not
playing the status game with the Corinthian elite. Have a listen:

> And so it was with me, brothers and sisters. When I came to you, I did
> not come with eloquence or human wisdom as I proclaimed to you the
> testimony about God. For I resolved to know nothing while I was with
> you except Jesus Christ and him crucified. I came to you in weakness
> with great fear and trembling. My message and my preaching were
> not with wise and persuasive words, but with a demonstration of the
> Spirit's power, so that your faith might not rest on human wisdom,
> but on God's power. (2:1–5)

This is why Paul didn't come with a great display of oratory, trying
to impress people with 'brand Paul'. It was to ensure that their
response to the gospel wasn't based on human cleverness or intellectual appeal – but on the power of God. He didn't want their faith
to be a result of human persuasive skill or marketing spin. He wanted

to make it clear that it was the supernatural work of God. Again, so that no-one could boast.

If we're not careful, we can end up doing the *opposite* of what God does. Instead of embracing the 'foolishness' of the gospel, we pimp it until it looks just like the wisdom of the world. We sugar-coat it with what people want to hear. We tailor it so that it panders to the pretensions of our society and speaks to people's 'felt needs'. Don't do that. Paul steadfastly refused to do it. God has *always* refused to do it – because he wants us to realize that salvation is *from him*, by *his* power. It's not from ourselves, so that no-one can boast.

Conclusion: Don't bring your pretensions to church!

When you look at it that way, how *foolish* it is for God's people to be divided over such lame status symbols as speaking style, wealth, intelligence or popularity – or any of the other values our status-grasping world holds dear. God doesn't work that way. Paul didn't work that way. Neither should we.

> Show how this passage relates to the *propositio* about unity.

Today's passage tells us to get rid of our pretensions.

That's the first step in ridding the church of division and rivalry: stop being concerned about our public image, our claim to superiority. Instead, trust in the power of God and his gospel. Get rid of the bling, and get back to the cross.

10. PREACHING PATHOS

For decades, marketers have been taught: *sell the sizzle, not the steak.* Major on the benefits of the product, or the emotions related to it, rather than the product itself and its features. The family's primary caregiver is sold staple items like margarine and bread by focusing less on the actual products and more on the approving reactions of their grateful family. Men are sold women's jewellery mostly by ignoring the jewellery itself in favour of her reaction to being given it. And when it comes to things like perfume and men's cologne, the tangible features are almost impossible to sell via electronic media; so until someone invents SmellaVision™ we're going to be stuck with bewildering advertisements with no plotlines involving impossibly attractive people strutting in expensive suits and designer dresses looking confident, sultry and (from what I can make out) slightly constipated – which I'm guessing is the feeling you're supposed to get when you wear the scent in question. It's persuasion through emotion, not rational argument.

It happens in public speaking, too. In 2008 when Barack Obama declared, 'Yes we can!', he wasn't simply making the argument that his policies were achievable; he was inviting his audience to *feel* the audacious hope that was the centrepiece of his campaign. In 1963 when Martin Luther King had a dream, he wasn't just outlining a manifesto for racial equality; he wanted his audience to have an *emotional experience* of the alternative world his vision promised. In the first century, when Paul exclaimed:

> Oh, the depth of the riches of the wisdom and knowledge of God!
>> How unsearchable his judgments,
>> and his paths beyond tracing out!
> 'Who has known the mind of the Lord?
>> Or who has been his counsellor?'
> 'Who has ever given to God,
>> that God should repay them?'
> (Rom. 11:33–35)

he wasn't formulating a doctrinal statement on the attributes of God; he was moving his audience to praise by *evoking the emotions* his audience should feel when made freshly aware of the utter grandeur of God. Each rhetorical question demands the hearer respond with the answer, 'No-one!', and thus be drawn into Paul's expression of wonder and awe.[1]

These are all *pathos* arguments. They are appeals to the emotions – in particular, the stronger emotions such as love or hate, hope or fear, pity or disdain. The speakers might go about them in different ways; as we said before, Aristotle would try to evoke emotions by giving rational reasons why the audience should feel a certain way, whereas Roman writers like Cicero and Quintilian sought to move their audience through their use of words and imagery. Nevertheless, their aim was the same: to arouse strong feelings in the audience in order to persuade them.

Why did they want to do this? Because emotions initiate deliberation and provoke action. As Aristotle said: 'For the judgements we deliver *are not the same* when we are influenced by joy or sorrow,

---

1. Leander E. Keck, '*Pathos* in Romans? Mostly Preliminary Remarks', in Thomas H. Olbricht and Jerry L. Sumney (eds.), *Paul and Pathos* (Atlanta: SBL, 2001), p. 95.

love or hate';[2] 'The emotions are all those affections which cause men to *change their opinion* in regard to their judgements.'[3]

Paul explains it similarly. In 2 Corinthians, he refers to the previous, 'painful letter' and what it was intended to achieve:

> Even if I caused you sorrow by my letter, I do not regret it. Though I did regret it – I see that my letter hurt you, but only for a little while – yet now I am happy, not because you were made sorry, but because *your sorrow led you to repentance* . . . (2 Cor. 7:8–9a)

The letter was painful for Paul to write, but he didn't regret doing so because his pathos had the desired effect: it produced an emotion (sorrow) that led to a change in action (repentance).

Although pathos could be used anywhere throughout a speech, it was for this reason considered most appropriate in the *peroratio* (see chapter 8). This was the closing appeal, right at the point at which the audience were called upon to make their judgment. Your hearers had to be put in the right emotional state to be moved to action.

Identifying and preaching pathos

In applying this to preaching, the first step is, as always, to identify *where* the New Testament writer is using pathos, and *why*. In doing this, keep in mind the question of how feeling this particular emotion might work to persuade the audience of the epistle's *propositio*. And keep a lookout for the kinds of emotions that are commonly associated with each of the rhetorical genres.

In deliberative rhetoric, the most commonly evoked emotions are fear and hope:[4] the fearful consequences of *not* adopting the

---

2. Aristotle, *Rhetoric*, 1.2.5.

3. Ibid., 2.1.8.

4. Anders Eriksson, 'Fear of Eternal Damnation: *Pathos* Appeal in 1 Corinthians 15 and 16', in Thomas H. Olbricht and Jerry L. Sumney (eds.), *Paul and Pathos* (Atlanta: SBL, 2001), p. 116.

propositio are contrasted with the hopeful future that comes from accepting it. We find this frequently in Hebrews, where the writer refers to the fearsome consequences of 'falling away' or 'shrinking back', most famously in chapter 10:

> If we deliberately keep on sinning after we have received the knowledge of the truth, no sacrifice for sins is left, but only a fearful expectation of judgment and of raging fire that will consume the enemies of God . . . It is a dreadful thing to fall into the hands of the living God. (Heb. 10:26–27, 31)

Later, the writer contrasts the mountain of fear (Sinai) with the mountain of joy and hope (Zion):

> You have not come to a mountain that can be touched and that is burning with fire; to darkness, gloom and storm . . . The sight was so terrifying that Moses said, 'I am trembling with fear.' (12:18, 21)

> But you have come to Mount Zion, to the city of the living God, the heavenly Jerusalem. You have come to thousands upon thousands of angels in joyful assembly, to the church of the firstborn, whose names are written in heaven. (12:22–23a)

He associates these contrasting emotions with the two paths set before his audience: shrink back into the protection of the synagogue and remain at the foot of the mountain of fear, or persevere and join the multitude on the mountain of joy.

We also find this in 1 Peter, in which marginalized communities of believers are encouraged to remain loyal under suffering. The writer contrasts the fearful fate of those who persecute them – 'they will have to give account to him who is ready to judge the living and the dead' (4:5) – with the hope of 'an inheritance that can never perish, spoil or fade . . . kept in heaven for you' (1:4).

In epideictic rhetoric, the contrast is often between love and indignation:[5] the audience are encouraged to feel warmth towards

---

5. Ibid.

those who embrace the values being honoured, and indignation at those who oppose them. For example, in 1 John, the writer regularly evokes feelings of love and gratitude towards God and within his audience (e.g. 3:1; 4:7), contrasting with the arousing of indignation against the false teachers who have led people astray and then left the community (e.g. 2:19–20). In 2 Peter, the audience are even more strongly encouraged to be righteously angry with false teachers, who are the subject of an extended and particularly vitriolic invective in chapter 2.

Pathos in the text: pathos in the sermon

Once we've identified the presence and purpose of pathos in the text, we can then allow it to inform the tone and purpose of our sermon. If a biblical text was designed to evoke a particular emotion in its audience, shouldn't our sermon do likewise? Yet how often have you heard a text full of pathos preached in an emotionless, analytical way! Think of a pathos-rich passage like this one:

> Where, then, is your blessing of me now? I can testify that, if you could have done so, you would have torn out your eyes and given them to me. (Gal. 4:15)

A text full of emotion! Nevertheless, you can imagine the stereotype of a dry, expository preacher dealing with it, probably with his glasses sliding down onto the bridge of his nose: 'Paul here describes their former joy in an obviously hyperbolic fashion. The Greek word for "torn out" is particularly illuminating, as it's the same word used in Mark's Gospel for the friends of the paralytic digging through the roof . . .'[6] Don't *analyse* pathos passages: preach them with matching passion!

Yet it's not enough simply to preach pathos texts with matching emotion. We need to keep in mind *why* the biblical writer wanted to evoke that emotion in the light of his overall rhetorical purpose – because it won't always be appropriate in our own situation.

---

6. That's actually true.

For example, in 1 Corinthians 15 Paul uses the language of disadvantage ('useless', 'futile' and 'to be pitied') to set out the
consequences of denying a bodily resurrection (15:13–19). It's about
making his audience fear the long-term result of persisting in this
belief (i.e. it makes faith in Christ of no benefit), driving them to
change their thinking. That's not greatly different from how we might
preach this passage today, since there would be some – both inside
and outside the church – who might think similarly. So it might be
appropriate to use this strategy of evoking a sense of fear and hope-
lessness as a perfectly rational response to Paul's argument: *If you don't
believe in resurrection, what hope does that leave you with?* And then, along
with Paul, contrast it with the hope that the resurrection provides.[7]

By contrast, when Paul tries to evoke pity for himself in the first
two chapters of 2 Corinthians, how does that relate to us? Neither
Paul nor the original audience are part of our contemporary world,
and there isn't an obviously parallel situation. In the letter, Paul uses
pity as part of his aim to show that he's not a 'peddler of God's
word' for profit (2:17). He's not weak and indecisive (1:17), and given
their past history shouldn't have to commend himself to his audience
(3:1). It's hard, though, to see how evoking pity (for Paul, for the
preacher or for *anyone*) achieves anything in our own contemporary
situation. So the pathos of 2 Corinthians may well have to be left
back in the first century.

This is why we need to identify not just *where* the New Testament
writers use pathos, but also *why* – so we can work out whether it's
useful or not in the context of our sermon.

Finally, I'd also argue that our sermon should reflect the *kind* of
pathos argument being used in the text. Is it Aristotle's rational
approach, in which the audience is given logical reasons why they
should be feeling a particular emotion? Or is it the more affective
techniques of the later, Roman orators, through the choice of words
and images, and techniques such as comparison and hyperbole? We
see both in the New Testament texts.

---

7. For an excellent example of this, see Philip Yancey's sermon at his
   friend's funeral, partly reproduced in *Where Is God When It Hurts?*,
   rev. edn (Grand Rapids: Zondervan, 1990), pp. 269–272.

In fact, we see both in the pathos-rich letter to the Galatians, which is the subject of our next workshop.

Summary: When preaching pathos . . .

- Identify the emotions being evoked.
- Identify the type of pathos argument: Aristotle or the Latin writers?
- Match the pathos strategy of the sermon with the pathos strategy of the text.

Workshop: preaching pathos in Galatians 4:8–20

Pathos through rational argument

Let's take a look at Galatians 4:8–20, first as an example of pathos done Aristotle-style. Have a quick read of the passage now, thinking about the following questions:

1. What emotion(s) is the writer trying to arouse?
2. Why is he doing so, in the light of his overall rhetorical purpose?
3. Is this an appropriate strategy for our own context?

In a nutshell, Paul is trying to evoke in his audience anger or indignation towards the 'agitators' (as he calls them in 5:12) for misleading them, as well as a friendliness towards himself.

Why? In deliberative rhetoric, it often came down to which speaker you could *trust*. Paul wants his audience not to be taken in by the Judaizers' message (because they can't be trusted) and to remain loyal to him. Paul's argument will be most effective if he can arouse his audience to contrasting emotions towards his opponents and himself.

For us, it might be appropriate to arouse at least some feeling of indignation against those people or cultural forces which are trying to influence us to 'add to the gospel'. Often, in the name of Christian 'niceness', we overlook the devastating effects this can have on individuals and on whole denominations. A righteous anger might well be appropriate in this case. (We'll consider how it might be expressed in a culturally appropriate manner shortly.) Further, a helpful 'antidote' might be to rekindle feelings of warmth and loyalty towards God, towards the gospel message itself, and even towards those who first brought us that message.

So having answered a qualified 'yes' to the third question, we can then press further by asking:

1. How does *Paul* try to arouse these emotions? How might *we*, then, do the same?
2. How might we do the same, using the same (or similar) techniques found in the text?
3. Are Paul's techniques *appropriate* for our own context? Or do we need to use some different ones?

First, we notice that Paul hasn't just started the process in chapter 4 of Galatians. Right from the start of the letter he's been provocative, displaying his incredulity at how his audience, which he describes as having been 'bewitched' (3:1), could have been so misled by the Judaizers (1:6). We, too, might seek to provoke our hearers from the start by being more confrontational than usual in our style – pointing out with a degree of incredulity some examples of how susceptible we are to adding to the gospel of grace!

In the passage we're preaching on, Paul exposes the self-serving motives of those who would add legalistic requirements or cultural boundary markers to the gospel:

> Those people are zealous to win you over, but for no good. What they want is to alienate you from us, so that you may have zeal for them. (Gal. 4:17)

Likewise, we might expose the self-serving motives of present-day Judaizers: they want to define appropriate Christian conduct in their own image, according to their own preferences and prejudices. In this way, they are both protecting themselves from criticism and installing themselves as the models of piety. The gospel has become a means of gaining honour for themselves and marginalizing people who won't play along with this status game. This kind of offensive, selfish behaviour is the sort of thing about which we *should* be indignant, right? And the stakes are high: buying into their deception leads back into enslavement to idolatry (4:8–9). Paul wouldn't stand for it; *how dare we!*

Now, of course, we need to do this with cultural sensitivity. Invective and strong language are usually considered poor form in Western culture. Personal attacks are frowned upon as being immature and a sign that you're lacking in rational argument. (By contrast, in the first century, and particularly in Asia Minor, if you didn't do this, people wouldn't take you seriously.) So we tread carefully. We might need to soften 'anger' to 'indignation'. We might think about depersonalizing the source of the agitation to 'cultural forces'. We might not name names, but speak of the 'type of person' who pursues a modern-day Judaizing agenda. This may not convey Paul's strategy exactly, but it's perhaps a more culturally conditioned appropriation of it – and will probably achieve the same function in a culture that is mostly repelled by personal attack and bombast. We temper such rhetorical invective, as Paul did, in line with the cultural standards of the day, taking the edge off it where necessary. (And sometimes, as in the case of Paul's suggestion in Gal. 5:12 that his opponents go the whole way and castrate themselves, we might have to cut it out entirely.)

By contrast, Paul arouses feelings of friendship towards himself. He does this by using the language of friendship and kinship ('brothers and sisters', v. 12, as well as 'my dear children' in v. 19) and by reminding them of what he's done for them in the past which led to a close relationship and mutual affection:

> I plead with you, brothers and sisters, become like me, for I became like you. You did me no wrong. As you know, it was because of an illness that I first preached the gospel to you, and even though my illness was a trial to you, you did not treat me with contempt or scorn. Instead, you welcomed me as if I were an angel of God, as if I were Christ Jesus himself. Where, then, is your blessing of me now? I can testify that, if you could have done so, you would have torn out your eyes and given them to me. Have I now become your enemy by telling you the truth? (Gal. 4:12–16)

In short, Paul is saying: *I went to the trouble of becoming one of you (a Gentile, even though I myself am a Jew) in order to bring you the message*

*of salvation, demonstrating that I'm doing this for your benefit, not mine.
And you responded with great affection – back then, you would have
done anything for me! So what's changed? I'm still on your side!* In true
Aristotelian style, Paul's giving them some pretty good reasons to
have feelings of friendliness and loyalty towards him. He does
this so that they'll accept his rebuke and reject the message of the
agitators.

But how does that play out in our context? Friendliness towards
Paul is hardly a strategic objective of our sermon! Yet it's not hard
to see how the above rhetoric can be applied to God – who became
one of us, for our benefit – giving our hearers good reasons to feel
affection and loyalty towards God. *Think of the amazing grace God has
shown towards you – and how precious that grace appeared the hour you first
believed. Has anything changed? So listen to what God says, and reject the lies
that seek to enslave you all over again!*

Pathos through words and imagery

We can also look at this passage in Galatians from the perspective
of the later, Roman writers. Although Paul is primarily building up
a rational case to arouse indignation towards his opponents and
friendliness towards himself, his use of words also acts in a more
emotive way – techniques which are available to us, too.

In true deliberative fashion, he portrays in negative terms their
future if they continue to listen to his opponents' arguments: they
will again be 'enslaved' by 'weak and miserable forces' (4:9). How
might we describe today's Judaizing idols – of, say, prosperity, ecstatic
experience or denominational tradition – in ways that reveal their
true nature?

Again typically of deliberative rhetoric, Paul uses the emotion of
fear and the argument of disadvantage. He reveals his own 'fear'
that his work among them will have been 'wasted' (4:11). This
follows the advice of Cicero and Quintilian, which says that speakers
should themselves feel the emotions they want to evoke in their
hearers.[8] Are we afraid that there will be no eternal gain for those in
our congregation who are seduced by distortions of the gospel?

---

8. Cicero, *On Oratory*, 2.189; Quintilian, *Institutes of Oratory*, 6.2.26.

How can we convey this fear in a way that causes them to be (rightly) afraid of it, too?

To describe the Galatians' former response to and affection for him, Paul uses the technique of *hyperbole*. They received him as if he were 'an angel of God' or even 'Christ Jesus himself' (4:14), and they would have 'torn out' their own eyes to give them to Paul (4:15). How could we elicit the same kinds of emotions our audience felt when they first responded to the gospel?

In this passage, Paul also seeks to evoke pity (i.e. a strong sense of sympathy) for himself and his cause, presenting himself as the 'underdog' and the object of mistreatment. He's been unjustly treated by the Judaizers, as they want to 'alienate' Paul from the Galatians (4:17), as well as by the Galatians themselves, given their change of attitude towards him to the point where he could be considered an 'enemy' (4:16). Despite this, he's still acting for their good, just as he always has been, with deep, parental affection: it's as if he's going through the pain of having to birth them all over again (4:19). He doesn't seem to know what to do (4:20), perhaps following Quintilian's advice to 'feign . . . to be at a loss where to begin or end, or what to say in preference to something else, or whether we ought to speak at all'[9] as a way of arousing sympathy. And at the end of his letter, Paul pulls out all the stops (as you'd expect in a *peroratio*). Just like in a famous trial, when the speaker concluded his defence by ripping apart the defendant's tunic to expose the scars that testified to his brave service for his country,[10] Paul concludes by 'exposing' his own scars earned in service of Christ:

> From now on, let no one cause me trouble, for I bear on my body the marks of Jesus. (Gal. 6:17)

9. Quintilian, *Institutes*, 9.2.19. See Steven J. Kraftchik, 'Πάθη in Paul: The Emotional Logic of "Original Argument"', in Thomas H. Olbricht and Jerry L. Sumney (eds.), *Paul and Pathos* (Atlanta: SBL, 2001), p. 66.

10. Antonius' defence of Manius Aquilius, described by Cicero in *On Oratory*, 2.124.

Although evoking pity for Paul is not particularly relevant for our own situation, remember that in Galatians Paul is making the case for his 'client' – God and his gospel – against the opponents who sought to distort it. So it might be appropriate to evoke sympathy not for how *Paul* was treated by his opponents in the first century, but for how God and his gospel are treated today. We might portray the true gospel as the 'underdog', as it always has to battle our natural tendencies to redefine salvation as something we've earned or something we deserve. We might describe the affront caused to God by those who would consider being swayed by such distortions of the gospel, after all he has done for us. Indeed, we might tear open Christ's tunic to reveal his scars for us – the scars of the one who continues to be in the pains of childbirth while we are formed in him. And we might even communicate in our own tone some of the perplexity Paul felt over how to address this issue. In short, we reflect the intent of the text by evoking sympathy for God by an appeal to justice: *How could you ever consider doing this to God by distorting his gospel, after all he's done for you?*

A concluding word: pathos and manipulation

After reading this chapter, you've probably got a question forming in your mind: At what point does this kind of emotional persuasion become *manipulation*? Good question. (So good, in fact, that I've anticipated it and already prepared a *refutatio*.)

I'm sure we've all witnessed preaching events which have been emotionally manipulative – whether it be the words used, the stories told or even the surrounding environment. I clearly remember as an older teenager attending a large evangelistic rally in which background music was used in this way (I was hyper-alert to it, as I'd just finished a 'psychology of music' subject as part of my music degree). As the preacher prepared to call for a response, the band began quiet music, beginning at the tempo of a person's resting heartbeat, then gradually increasing. The chord changes were initially slow, and they also quickened, without providing any harmonic resolution. As the speed and volume built, and the music sounded as if it was about to resolve, tension in the room increased – only to be left unresolved, as the music slipped sideways and went back to being soft and slow (an interrupted cadence – moving to the relative minor – for any musicians reading this). This whole process happened three times, until the preacher finally called for people to come forward. At that point, the harmony was resolved, the ten minutes or so of musical tension was suddenly released, and hundreds of people streamed forward to 'receive Christ'. I was left wondering how many responded to the gospel that night, and how many simply responded to the emotion of the music.

That's why I never use background music during the *peroratio* of my sermons. As preachers of the gospel, we want to avoid manipulation. It disrespects the free will God gave humanity and shows a lack of trust in God's effectual calling.

For this reason, some want to go to the other extreme and avoid all kinds of persuasive strategies (other than, perhaps, the rational *logos* approach). Some do so out of a wariness of emotion, or even out of prejudice against it. This goes all the way back to Plato, who viewed the emotions as irrational, belonging to the material, inferior existence; so pathos was an inferior strategy for persuasion. Yet even he recognized he was in the minority, and in later works reluctantly conceded its effectiveness for persuasion, while still opposing its use to manipulate.[11]

Others oppose emotional persuasion on ideological grounds, seeing it as inherently hierarchical and manipulative.[12] Yet this doesn't have to be the case, as Hogan has shown by drawing a careful distinction between ethical persuasion and manipulation.[13] She uses Williamson and Allen's definition of the two to show the difference:

---

11. Thomas H. Olbricht, '*Pathos* as Proof in Greco-Roman Rhetoric', in Thomas H. Olbricht and Jerry L. Sumney (eds.), *Paul and Pathos* (Atlanta: SBL, 2001), p. 12.

12. See e.g. Lucy Atkinson Rose, *Sharing the Word: Preaching in the Roundtable Church*, 1st edn (Louisville: Westminster John Knox Press, 1997), pp. 14–16.

13. Lucy Lind Hogan, 'Rethinking Persuasion: Developing an Incarnational Theology of Preaching', *Homiletic* 24, no. 2 (1999), p. 5.

'A manipulator attempts to convince others that their freedom is much more limited than it really is', whereas 'the persuader offers the persuadee an option in the hope that the one who receives the option will evaluate the option critically and will respond to it in the full knowledge of other options and the strengths and weaknesses of all the options'.[14]

Paul draws a similar distinction, using rhetorical strategies throughout 1 Corinthians while explicitly avoiding the kind of rhetoric that *could* be manipulative – so that any response is due to the power of the gospel itself (1 Cor. 2:5). By contrast, using persuasive techniques that have been 'focus grouped' to appeal to human pretensions and desires is characteristic of false teaching (e.g. Rom. 16:18; 2 Tim. 4:3–4).

As we've seen throughout this chapter, the New Testament writers themselves use pathos to persuade their audiences, sometimes quite explicitly (e.g. 2 Cor. 7, noted above). This alone should argue against throwing the persuasive baby out with the manipulative bathwater (babies can be very effective persuaders). As Buttrick observes, it is 'emphatically unnatural' to be unpersuasive and unemotional when preaching the gospel.[15] Instead, we'd do well to adopt 'a rhetorical stance that balances *pathos* with *ethos* and *logos*, creating sermons that move rather than manipulate. *Pathos* prepares the listeners, but it's not an end in itself.'[16]

In short, pathos should be used in sermons *where the biblical text itself uses pathos*, and with great care to avoid crossing over into manipulation.

---

14. Clark Willamson and Ronald Allen, *Adventures of the Spirit: A Guide to Worship from the Perspective of Process Theology* (Lanham: New York University Press, 1997), pp. 117–118, cited in Hogan, 'Rethinking Persuasion', p. 6.

15. David Buttrick, *Homiletic: Moves and Structures* (Philadelphia: Fortress, 1987), p. 77.

16. Lucy Lind Hogan and Robert Reid, *Connecting with the Congregation: Rhetoric and the Art of Preaching* (Nashville: Abingdon Press, 1999), p. 71.

Exercise

Read Hebrews 12:18–28.

- What emotion(s) is the author seeking to evoke? Why?
- How might you preach this passage in line with its (emotive) function?

11. PREACHING LOGOS

In some ways, this final chapter will be the most straightforward. It's about *logos* – persuasion by rational argument – and, for many preachers, it's the mode in which we're most comfortable and with which we're most familiar. This is particularly the case in the West, with its rationalist heritage that can be traced back through the Enlightenment, through medieval scholasticism, right back to the dualism of Plato that proclaimed the superiority of the spiritual over the material, and therefore the rational over the emotional. We 'get' the fundamentals of logical argument.

Possibly for this reason it's also the focus of most commentaries: the logic of the text and what it's trying to *say*. So we don't need a chapter here to rehash two millennia of biblical scholarship. Moreover, although a study of the logos of a text is absolutely essential for the kind of quality exegesis that should underpin any expository sermon, there's less *preaching-specific* application to be gained than from our look at ethos and pathos. So this chapter will be a little less detailed than the previous two, without in any way suggesting that logos is less important to our understanding of the text or to the preaching of a persuasive sermon. The focus will be on simply recognizing the different kinds of rational proofs found in Scripture, and being able to adapt these proofs where necessary so that they function in a similar way within our own culture.

There were two kinds of arguments – or 'proofs' – in classical rhetorical theory. Let's get acquainted with both of them now.

Inartificial proofs

These days the word 'artificial' often suggests something that's false or less than genuine. At its heart, though, the word simply means something that's been constructed (an 'artifice'). In rhetoric, an *in*artificial proof was an argument that speakers didn't have to construct themselves; it was a given. This might be the citation of an accepted authority (such as a Greek poet, which Paul famously does in Acts 17:28) or the testimony of a witness (just as Peter called Barnabas and Paul to the stand to give evidence in support of his speech at the Jerusalem Council, in Acts 15:12).

Citation of an accepted authority
In the New Testament, the most frequently used type of inartificial proof is the citation of an accepted authority: the Hebrew Scriptures (every citation of or allusion to the Old Testament) and the words of Jesus.[1] This happens on almost every page of the New Testament and is dealt with at length by the commentaries. In preaching these texts, we need to ask whether the authority the New Testament author cites is *known, understood* and *accepted* among our own audience; if not, it might not function in the same way.

---

1. You want examples? Just read Romans; or Hebrews; or any epistle, really. Old Testament citations and allusions abound! And the words of Jesus are used, too: e.g. in 1 Cor. 11 Paul recites the words of institution of the Lord's Supper, and James frequently alludes to Jesus' teachings in the Sermon on the Mount. For a table of the latter, see David A. deSilva, *An Introduction to the New Testament: Contexts, Methods and Ministry Formation* (Downers Grove: InterVarsity Press, 2004), p. 817.

First, the authority might not be *known* by our hearers as well as it was by the original audience. Our congregation might not even pick up that the Old Testament is being quoted unless there is a clear introductory formula (e.g. 1 Cor. 1:31). Sometimes the allusions are so obscure that without commentaries we might not notice them ourselves (such as Job's hope of vindication in Job 13:16 being alluded to by Paul in Phil. 1:19). Our first task might simply be to point out the fact that the Hebrew Scriptures are being cited!

Second, the authority might not be as well *understood*. The New Testament authors often used a shorthand method of referring to a text, knowing that the audience would be familiar with its context. It's more likely that we'll have to explain all of this – the literary, historical and even canonical context – to our less biblically literate congregations. By showing *how* the New Testament writer applies the text for a new rhetorical situation, we make the source of authority not just known, but also *understood*.

Third, the authority itself might not be universally *accepted* by our audience. This would most obviously occur in evangelistic preaching, but not exclusively then. So if we're preaching on a New Testament text that cites the Hebrew Scriptures as an authority (as opposed to using them simply for an illustration) and many in our audience do *not* hold them to be authoritative, our sermon may *not* be doing what the biblical text was doing! (As I just noted, even Paul used different sources of authority when preaching to an audience of Greek philosophers, citing Stoic poets in Acts 17:28.) In such a case, we can either spend time arguing for the authority of Scripture – easier said than done in the middle of an evangelistic sermon – or place far less weight on the citation in the persuasive strategy of our sermon.

Eyewitness testimony

The other type of inartificial proof found frequently in the New Testament is that of eyewitness testimony. The most significant is, of course, testimony about Jesus' resurrection. Paul cites such existing testimony at length in 1 Corinthians 15:3–7, before adding his own (in v. 8). It's found in the key speeches in Acts by Peter, Stephen and Paul, and even as the climax of Paul's argument among pagan philosophers (17:31). John refers to this testimony as the basis for his authority to address his audience (1 John 1:1–4).

When we preach on such texts, we need to show how they functioned *as eyewitness accounts*. Although the texts – and their original rhetorical contexts – are almost two thousand years old, they can still function as eyewitness testimony to the truth of Jesus' resurrection, and therefore to the truth of the gospel message on which it's based.

Artificial proofs

The second type of argument is that which speakers had to construct for themselves: *artificial* proofs. Aristotle further divided these into deductive and inductive.

Deductive proofs

Deductive proofs are those which *deduce* a logical conclusion from a set of established propositions. The rhetorical handbooks gave a variety of forms for such arguments; we'll quickly look at two, just to get the idea[2] (and I won't bother you with much of the terminology, as that's a bit of a mess; for example, the term *enthymeme* could be used by Aristotle to refer to one kind of argument, and by Quintilian to refer to another[3]).

Arguments drawn from incompatibles

The simplest was an argument in which two ideas or behaviours were shown to be logically incompatible. These were usually expressed as rhetorical questions, sometimes chained together, and they often contained an implied air of incredulity:[4]

---

2. There are plenty more: see chapter 8 of my *Preaching the New Testament as Rhetoric: The Promise of Rhetorical Criticism for Expository Preaching*, Australian College of Theology Monograph Series (Eugene: Wipf & Stock, 2014).

3. David Aune tries to make sense of it all in his corrective article 'The Use and Abuse of the Enthymeme in New Testament Scholarship', *New Testament Studies* 48 (2003), pp. 299–320.

4. See Paul A. Holloway, 'The Enthymeme as an Element of Style in Paul', *Journal of Biblical Literature* 120, no. 2 (2001), pp. 329–343.

After beginning by means of the Spirit, are you now trying to finish by means of the flesh? (Gal. 3:3)

You, then, who teach others, do you not teach yourself? You who preach against stealing, do you steal? You who say that people should not commit adultery, do you commit adultery? You who abhor idols, do you rob temples? (Rom. 2:21–22)

Or do you not know that the Lord's people will judge the world? And if you are to judge the world, are you not competent to judge trivial cases? (1 Cor. 6:2)

As preachers, we seek to convey the rhetorical function of these questions to our own hearers. We might think about how to express them in ways that will more powerfully bring home the inconsistencies in our own society's behaviour, or even in our own congregation. For example, in preaching Galatians 3:3 we could ask our audience: 'Having started with the Spirit, have you now come to rely on your Christian service, or church attendance, or all the stuff you've learned *about* God over the years?' Or in preaching 1 Corinthians 6:3 we might even be bold enough to ask: 'If we're going to judge the world, can we not run our church business meetings in a civil manner?'

Arguments drawn from logical syllogisms
A more complicated pattern was based on the classical syllogism that was the foundation of Greek logic. In a syllogism, a general statement (the major premise) is combined with a specific statement (the minor premise) to deduce a conclusion. The most famous one is:

Major premise: All men are mortal.
Minor premise: Socrates is a man.
Conclusion: Therefore, Socrates is mortal.

We see an example of this in 1 Corinthians 13:8–10:

Major: All imperfect things will pass away when a perfect form comes (v. 10).

Minor: At present, prophecies, tongues and knowledge are imperfect (v. 9).
Conclusion: Prophecies, tongues and knowledge will pass away (v. 8).[5]

However, most of the time the New Testament writers (in line with Aristotle's advice) use a shortened form of syllogism in which one of the three elements is implied.[6] The audience have to 'fill in' the missing element, either because it's so obvious that to state it would be too tedious, or as a way of making the audience invest in the argument and its conclusion by being invited to put the logic together themselves.[7] So we might well say: 'Socrates is mortal, because all men are mortal' – the conclusion followed by the major premise – trusting our audience to work out the (rather obvious) minor premise that Socrates is a man. We see the same pattern in Galatians 3:28: 'There is neither Jew nor Greek [conclusion] . . . for you are all one in Christ Jesus [major premise].' Paul omits the minor premise: namely, that Jews and Greeks are not one, but are distinct peoples.

So what does this mean for our preaching? First, realize that most of the time New Testament syllogisms will be incomplete. In exegeting the text it's a helpful discipline to reconstruct the implied premise. It forces us to make the logic explicit and assists us in mapping out the flow of argument. And, quite significantly, it helps us identify the cultural and theological assumptions of the audience that might be implied in the omitted element of the syllogism.[8]

---

5. Marc J. Debanné, *Enthymemes in the Letters of Paul*, T & T Clark Library of Biblical Studies (London: T & T Clark, 2006), p. 535.

6. These are often called *enthymemes*, because part of the argument has to be supplied 'in the mind' of the listener (*thymos* = 'mind'). However, be aware that the term *enthymeme* is used by some ancient writers to refer to arguments drawn from incompatibles, or to expanded syllogisms (more usually called *epicheiremes*) in which a reason is given to support each of the premises. Trust me, it's best just not to go there.

7. Debanné, *Enthymemes*, p. 26; Michael Morrison, *Enthymemes in Hebrews*, Kindle Edition (Amazon Digital Services, 2010), p. 22.

8. Morrison, *Enthymemes in Hebrews*, p. 3.

This can be crucial in preaching, as our audience might *not* share those assumptions, and might miss the logic. For example:

> Galatians 3:25–26: [Conclusion] Now that this faith has come, we are no longer under a guardian. [minor premise] So in Christ Jesus you are all children (Greek: 'sons') of God through faith.

Here, the major premise is omitted: the cultural practice of being called a 'son' when a person came of age and was freed from the guardianship of a pedagogue. This probably needs to be made explicit to contemporary audiences, but of course needed no such explanation in the original setting.

Now let's take a more complicated example, from 1 Thessalonians 2:3–6. We can summarize the logic as follows:

> Major premise (implied): Only people who seek human approval deceive, flatter and come with impure motives.
> Minor premise (vv. 5–6): We are not coming with deceit or flattery, and our motives are pure.
> Conclusion (vv. 3–4): Therefore, we don't seek human approval.[9]

The major premise may require some explanation to a contemporary audience, as we don't share the same social background. As Bruce puts it, the Greek world was full of 'wandering charlatans . . . peddling their religious or philosophical nostrums, and living at the expense of their devotees'.[10] On the one hand, this is far enough removed from our experience that we'll need to explain the background to our congregation. Yet, on the other hand, it's not hard to see some similarities with our own culture: the secular and religious 'gurus' who peddle their ideas in books or seminars, and are widely seen to be in it for the money or status. In both settings, Christian ministry ought to be seen to be in stark contrast to the profit-seeking charlatans so prevalent in the wider world. By

---

9. Debanné, *Enthymemes*, p. 393.
10. F. F. Bruce, *1 and 2 Thessalonians*, Word Biblical Commentary (Dallas: Word, 1982), p. 26.

explicitly dealing with the implied major premise, it helps us apply it more incisively.

There is danger, however, in overanalysing (or, more accurately, in allowing too much of our exegetical analysis to end up in the sermon, rather than on the cutting-room floor where it belongs). Remember that the rhetorical effect of these shortened syllogisms was to make the audience participate by filling in the gaps. If we always make the missing elements explicit, we may well be robbing the arguments of their rhetorical force. So, if the implied element doesn't need explanation, *don't explain it!* And if it does, think about explaining the background first; then present the shortened syllogism and let the audience join the dots themselves.

Finally, our analysis should also keep us focused on the conclusion (not the premises) as the rhetorical intent of the text. So as we preach, we apply the conclusion, not the premises. For example, in preaching 2 Corinthians 12:14 we won't apply 'children should not have to save up for their parents, but parents for their children' as a timeless principle.[11] For a start, it may not be a value shared in all cultures! And Paul's purpose here isn't to argue for the premise, but to *use* the premise (which his culture holds to be true) in support of his conclusion: that he won't be a burden to his 'children' in Christ. Identifying the structure of deductive proofs in this way focuses us on the rhetorical intent of the argument.

Inductive proofs

Inductive proofs are those that *induce* an answer from previously observed examples or patterns. The two main categories of inductive proof are analogies and examples.[12] Analogies are drawn from general observations of the world: more specifically, according to Quintilian, from the 'actions of men' as well as 'from dumb animals and inanimate objects'.[13] Examples, by contrast, are drawn from specific people or events – either in history or in the contemporary world.

---

11. So we can't use this verse to claim that the Bible tells parents not to blow their children's inheritance on cruises and caravans.

12. See Aristotle, *Rhetoric*, 2.20.3–5.

13. Quintilian, *Institutes of Oratory*, 5.11.23.

Inductive proofs were particularly suitable for deliberative rhetoric. And since the majority of the New Testament epistles are deliberative, it's no surprise that we find many such inductive proofs.

Analogies are a dime a dozen; here are some we can find just in 1 Corinthians:

- The world of humans: child-rearing (3:2), building (3:10–15), soldiering and farming (3:6–9; 9:7) and athletics (9:24–27);
- The natural world: fields (3:9), yeast (5:6), the created order (15:38–41) and the human body (12:12–27);
- Inanimate objects: buildings (3:9, 16–17) and musical instruments (14:7–8).

Analogies were often quite stereotyped: there was a common stock of them you could draw upon, depending on your subject matter. It's a bit like the way stand-up comedians of the 1990s would have a stock of standard jokes involving the poor quality of airline food, the gender-relationship minefield and interactions with crazy taxi drivers (I'm looking at you, Jerry Seinfeld). If you were urging hard work and discipline, talk about soldiers and athletes. If you thought people were being immature, mention that it's about time they moved on to solid food. If you wanted a group of diverse people to unite for the common good, use the analogy of the various parts of the human body.[14]

Examples are a little less frequent, but often more extended. They were commonly drawn from Israel's history; for example:

- In Galatians 3 and Romans 4, Paul uses the example of Abraham to induce that righteousness is by faith, apart from law.
- In 1 Corinthians 10:1–13, the example of Israel's disobedience is described explicitly by Paul as a 'type' (*typos*) or pattern to instruct his audience.

---

14. Although Paul did this in e.g. 1 Cor. 12, Rom. 12 and Col. 1:18, it was a common metaphor for civic unity. See e.g. Epictetus, *Discourses*, 2.5.35; Seneca, *Moral Epistles*, 2.31.7; and especially Livy, *History of Rome*, 2.32.12.

- Hebrews 11 provides a string of examples of people from
  history who ignored the shaming of the wider world in the
  light of the greater reward on offer, culminating in the
  example of Jesus himself (12:1–4).

They were also drawn from people personally known to author
and audience:

- In 1 Corinthians, Paul famously uses his own example (11:1),
  especially in how he seeks the advantage of others instead of
  his own (10:33).
- In Philippians, Paul begins with his own example (1:12–26;
  also 3:17), moving on to that of Christ (2:5–11) and his
  valued co-workers Timothy and Epaphroditus (2:19–30).
  These are contrasted with the examples of Paul's rival
  preachers (1:15–18), Paul's 'warped and crooked generation'
  (2:15), the Judaizers (3:2–6, 18–20) and Euodia and Syntyche
  (4:2–3).
- The past example of the audience themselves is used in
  Hebrews 10:32–35 as a way of urging action in the future.

So how does this help our preaching?

Most simply, it gives us ideas for illustrations. To a certain
extent, it *gives us* the illustrations, which we can then expand
or adapt if we like. Paul's agricultural imagery in 1 Corinthians 3
could spark any number of gardening stories – or even some interesting stories, for that matter. The body analogy probably works
just as well today, advances in prosthetics notwithstanding.
The example of Abraham's faith – cited in numerous places –
remains a relevant paradigm for faith. Where the New Testament
provides us with analogies and examples, we use them to illustrate
our sermons.

However, it won't always be quite so straightforward. As we saw
earlier, many of the analogies were commonplaces: drawn from a
standard stock of images familiar to the audience and part of their
everyday lives. So while we might *understand* the images, not all of
them will connect with our lived experience at that primal level. We
might 'get' farming analogies, but for most Western city-dwellers

farming is not a direct part of their lives. The content remains intelligible, but the rhetorical effect is somewhat muted.

To address this, we'll need to play with the analogies in the text – even invent new ones. We might have Paul and Apollos playing different positions on the same sporting team, in which the winger cannot say to the half back, 'I don't need you'. We might build on the foundation of Christ with bricks, in contrast to wood and straw, since 'The Three Little Pigs' has become part of our shared story heritage. That's the fun, creative part of preaching! And it's important to do it if we want our imagery to function *as commonplaces* in our own world, not just in the world of the first century.

We might also need to translate – or more fully explain – some of the historical examples, too, if we suspect a general lack of Old Testament literacy in our congregation. And we'll need to find contemporary examples worthy of imitation, in addition to those found in the text (such as Paul, Timothy and Epaphroditus) who are no longer personally known to us. However, we've already talked about that in our discussion of 'Whose ethos?' in chapter 9, so let's move on.

Summary: Types of logos argument

Inartificial proofs: e.g. citation of an authority, testimony
Artificial proofs:
  • Deductive: e.g. argument from incompatibles; syllogisms
  • Inductive: e.g. analogies and examples
When preaching a logos text, translate the effect of the proof(s) into the culture of the audience.

Some general observations about logos

In this chapter, we've looked at the major types of rational proof we encounter in the New Testament: those which already exist, such as citations of Scripture and eyewitness testimony, and those that have to be constructed by the author, such as syllogisms, analogies and examples. We need to be able to identify these in order to understand the logical strategy of the text, and to translate (where necessary) those arguments more appropriately for our own culture.

However, we can also glean some general principles for preaching logos texts.

First, we see that the New Testament epistles aren't dogmatic assertions; they are reasoned argument. The authors, for the most part, don't command their audience to obey their instruction, but persuade them of the soundness of their advice. Make this an aim of your preaching: don't just state truth and demand obedience, but show *why* it's true and *why* it's beneficial to obey – all the more so if that's what the biblical text is doing!

Second, you may have picked up how many of the arguments begin with what was commonly believed by the audience: the authorities cited are those which were accepted by the audience; the examples are drawn from their history; the analogies are drawn from their everyday lives. The New Testament authors begin where their audience are, giving us yet another basis for preaching that is contextual and incarnational. Shouldn't our preaching follow their example? Use building blocks and examples which are commonly held among your audience – even if that may not fully correspond with the worldview of the original audience.

Third, the different types of logical argument we see in the New Testament were designed not just to be persuasive, but to be clear and memorable. This was particularly the case for maxims (sayings), syllogisms and analogies. When preaching from such material, don't let your (necessary) explanations detract from the clarity and memorability of the material.

Finally, we've seen that some of the forms were meant to engage the audience in the process of coming to the conclusion. The syllogism with an element missing asked the hearers to supply the missing part in their own minds. The argument from opposites asked pointed questions which, if answered honestly, would expose hypocrisy. Analogies and examples asked the audience to induce the answer from the pattern being given. Go, and do likewise. Involve your congregation in this kind of guided dialogue, leading them to discover the truth themselves.

Exercise

Go through a logos-rich text and identify the different types of argument (Hebrews is a fun place to start).

If you spot a shortened syllogism, identify the missing premise. Restate each part of the syllogism in your own words. You'll be surprised at how much clearer the argument becomes.[15]

---

15. For some worked examples of this in Hebrews, see Morrison, *Enthymemes in Hebrews* (available for £1 / $1 at Amazon).

GOT QUESTIONS?

Before you head out to catch some rhetorical waves, you might have a few questions. Here are some I'm often asked.

Is all this rhetorical stuff really going on in the New Testament epistles?

This is a good question to ask, and there isn't space to answer it in detail here. This book is more of a 'how to' guide than an answer to the question 'Is it right to be doing this?' I've given a very quick overview of the argument in Appendix A, but if you want to evaluate the method properly, see chapter 2 of my previous book.[1] As I said at the outset, this method of analysing New Testament epistles isn't mine, but is drawn from four decades of rhetorical scholarship; I'm just putting it to work to help with the task of preaching.

---

1. Tim MacBride, *Preaching the New Testament as Rhetoric: The Promise of Rhetorical Criticism for Expository Preaching*, Australian College of Theology Monograph Series (Eugene: Wipf & Stock, 2014).

How do I go about putting all of this into practice in my preaching?

The short answer is: not all in one go!

I've deliberately arranged the three parts of this book in the order you find them because it's the order in which I started applying it to my preaching as I 'discovered' rhetoric for myself as a seminary student.

Start with considering rhetorical genre (with the help of commentaries – see Appendix B). The next time you preach on an epistle, match the function of the genre to the function of your sermon.

Once you've explored genre for a few sermons, reread part 2. Identify the *propositio* (again, with the help of commentaries) and preach each part of an epistle in the light of the *propositio*. You'll find this starts to form your thinking about application.

Next, identify which part of the speech you're preaching on and see how its function might inform the function of your sermon.

Finally – and you might not get to this until a year's time, depending on how often you preach from the epistles – reread part 3. Try to put into practice some of the more technical concepts relating to ethos, pathos and logos.

Above all, don't try to learn this in the abstract (at least, I didn't, so that's the tip I'm passing on to you). As you preach on the epistles, gradually add more elements of rhetorical theory to your toolkit, and try catching a few shore-breakers in your sermons. After all, no-one learned to surf just by reading a book about it.

Do my congregation have to learn all this to understand the New Testament?

Often behind this question is the concern that we're setting up a body of specialist knowledge that's only available to the 'educated elite', excluding people from reading the New Testament for themselves. This is an important concern, and my response has two elements.

First, this wasn't specialist knowledge in the first century; it was common to everyone in that society. Basic rhetoric was taught to the educated classes even in primary school, and everyone was used to hearing (and evaluating) oratory as the primary medium of mass communication. It's just the same as how today, as consumers of film and television, we know the basics of how these media are supposed to function without having had to go to film school. So we're simply asking readers of the New Testament to get inside the cultural world of ordinary people living in the Roman Empire two thousand years ago.

Second, this happens already, to some extent. One of the fundamental tasks of preaching is exegesis – making the meaning understood. We wouldn't need to do this if everything could be understood at first reading. As preachers, we educate our congregations with all sorts of cultural information: descriptions of tax collectors and Pharisees, first-century farming practices and the role of women in the ancient world, to name just a few. And we do this to equip our hearers to understand properly Jesus' parables and the stories of his interactions with people. Further, there's a lot more background information that informs how we present the text but which may not be explicitly mentioned in our sermons: ideas such as Jewish messianic expectations, the old-covenant sacrificial system or the conventions of apocalyptic literature.

Rhetorical conventions of the first century are no different. They only feel as if they belong to a more specialist body of knowledge than some of this other cultural material because a few generations of biblical scholarship neglected them. It shouldn't be beyond most congregations to be educated every so often about rhetorical genre and the central proposition of an epistle – much as you might stop for a minute to explain what a Sadducee was. And *most* of the rhetorical analysis doesn't have to be made explicit in the sermon; rather, it's there to guide the preacher's construction of the message in the study. (See the sample sermon on Ephesians 2 at the end of chapter 3 for one of the occasional times I've made the rhetoric explicit in a sermon.)

Does this apply to other biblical genres?

Yes and no.

It doesn't apply in the detail we've gone into in this book. Epistles, as written speeches, follow the conventions of the speech-writing handbooks of the day, so we can be quite detailed and explicit in our analysis. We can do similarly with how Luke follows the stated historiographical conventions of, say, Thucydides, in writing Acts. For the most part, though, there weren't similar handbooks on how to write apocalyptic or a gospel; we just infer the rhetorical strategies from the content and by comparing them with similar works from the same period. So we can't form as structured an approach.

Having said that, the general principle of having the sermon say *and do* what the text says *and does* is still appropriate for all of Scripture. And I still follow that principle in preaching all the other biblical genres, looking for the original function of the text and aligning my sermon with it. I just don't have any rhetorical handbooks to guide me, so I have to be a little more cautious about my conclusions.

Time for some waves

But enough questions. Enough theory. You'll never catch any waves unless you step into the water. Plan a series through an epistle sometime soon. (If you're paralysed by choice, Philippians is a good one to start with.) Try some of this out. You may fall off the board sometimes, but that's half the fun. And when you *do* find your sermon being driven along by the rhetoric of the text, there's no better feeling.

Go catch some waves.

APPENDIX A: THEORETICAL JUSTIFICATION

This appendix is a very brief summary of the justification for applying the rhetorical-critical method to New Testament epistles. If you want to evaluate the rationale for this methodology properly, please see chapter 2 of my earlier book, upon which this discussion is based.[1]

Various approaches to rhetorical criticism

First, however, if we take a look at the landscape of what's called 'rhetorical criticism' we'll see that the term covers a variety of approaches. From the time of Augustine, through the Renaissance under figures such as Melanchthon, and even up until the middle of the last century, rhetorical analysis of the New Testament had a very narrow focus, looking mainly at rhetorical 'style' – essentially, a focus

---

1. Tim MacBride, *Preaching the New Testament as Rhetoric: The Promise of Rhetorical Criticism for Expository Preaching*, Australian College of Theology Monograph Series (Eugene: Wipf & Stock, 2014).

on figures of speech. The genre and arrangement of material was all but ignored.[2] In 1968, however, James Muilenburg used his presidential address to the Society of Biblical Literature to introduce the term 'rhetorical criticism' to a wider audience, and to define it more in terms of structure than ornamentation.[3] He called upon other scholars to explore this redefined field, and many answered his call over the subsequent decades.[4]

Predictably, different approaches were taken. Although any movement defies simplistic analysis, Stanley Porter, in his introduction to the papers presented at the 1992 Heidelberg conference, identifies the fundamental division:

> For some rhetoric means the categories used by the ancients, as reflected in the classical orators or in the handbooks on rhetoric, or in some combination of both. For others rhetoric means rhetorical categories developed in subsequent times and places, in particular the categories of the European New Rhetoricians of this century.[5]

Despite the obvious diversity which exists within each of these two 'schools', the approaches within each group share some

---

2. For a helpful overview, see William Wuellner, 'Where Is Rhetorical Criticism Taking Us?', *Catholic Biblical Quarterly* 49 (1987), pp. 449–451; J. Murphy, *Rhetoric in the Middle Ages: A History of Rhetorical Theory from St Augustine to the Renaissance* (Berkeley: University of California Press, 1974), pp. 47–63; and Carl J. Classen, *Rhetorical Criticism of the New Testament* (Boston: Brill, 2002), pp. 114–115.

3. James Muilenburg, 'Form Criticism and Beyond', *Journal of Biblical Literature* 88 (1969), pp. 1–18.

4. For a comprehensive survey of works in the field, see Duane F. Watson and Alan J. Hauser, *Rhetorical Criticism of the Bible: A Comprehensive Bibliography with Notes on History and Method*, Biblical Interpretation Series (Leiden: Brill, 1994).

5. Stanley E. Porter and Thomas H. Olbricht (eds.), *Rhetoric and the New Testament: Essays from the 1992 Heidelberg Conference*, Journal for the Study of the New Testament Supplement Series, vol. 90 (Sheffield: Sheffield Academic Press, 1993), p. 21.

fundamental philosophical and methodological assumptions which set it apart from the other. The first style of approach seeks to analyse rhetoric according to classical Graeco-Roman terminology and theory, with historical concerns uppermost in mind.[6] Although this school began by using the ancient rhetorical handbooks, it expanded to include lessons drawn from looking at the actual speeches themselves.[7] The second type employs more universal categories drawn from a diverse range of social-scientific and linguistic fields, and is essentially a form of literary analysis.[8] (Stamps includes a third grouping which he calls a 'hybrid' of the two.[9] Methodologically, however, this is best viewed as a more moderate form of the second category, as it goes beyond classical theory, despite maintaining more of an interest in historical questions. This is undoubtedly a significant and important subdivision to make, but is not as philosophically fundamental.)

It's precisely the imposition of 'modern analytical categories on the text which the NT writers neither knew nor used'[10] which leads me to avoid using the 'new' rhetorical approaches in expository

---

6. Key figures who take this approach are Hans-Dieter Betz, whose rhetorically based commentary on Galatians was programmatic for the 'historical' school; the classicist George Kennedy; Margaret Mitchell; and, more recently, Ben Witherington III.

7. Margaret M. Mitchell, *Paul and the Rhetoric of Reconciliation* (Louisville: Westminster John Knox Press, 1993), pp. 6–10.

8. The more modern school draws from the more universal rhetorical theories of those such as Chaim Perelman and Lucie Olbrechts-Tyteca, and Kenneth Burke; leading exponents include Wilhelm Wuellner and Vernon Robbins.

9. Dennis L. Stamps, 'Rhetorical Criticism of the New Testament: Ancient and Modern Evaluations of Argumentation', in Stanley E. Porter and David Tombs (eds.), *Approaches to New Testament Study*, Journal for the Study of the New Testament Supplement Series (Sheffield: Sheffield Academic Press, 1995), p. 135.

10. Ben Witherington III, *New Testament Rhetoric: An Introductory Guide to the Art of Persuasion in and of the New Testament* (Eugene: Cascade, 2009), p. 242.

preaching. This is because their aim is not to create an objective approach to recovering the original intent or function of the text. In fact, the exponents of these approaches tend not to be as interested in such historical questions of intent. They're more concerned with the rhetorical function of the text in our contemporary social context, particularly as it relates to the exercise of power and oppression.[11] The fundamental questions being asked are not to do with what a text originally *did* and what it *therefore* does now, but what we can *make* it do for our *own present agenda.*

This is why I restrict myself in this book to the methods of the 'historical' school of rhetorical criticism, since they fit with the purpose of *expository* preaching from an evangelical framework. As Brian Peterson concludes:

> The study of these ancient texts is first of all an historical task, and for most scholars who study these texts it does matter what Paul intended to communicate and accomplish with those original hearers. Rhetorical analysis of these texts requires a referent within the world of Paul and his churches, and the Greco-Roman rhetorical tradition, embodied both in the handbooks and speeches, provides that referent.[12]

The appropriateness of rhetorical criticism for the study of the epistles

In applying the historical approach to New Testament texts there are two critical objections to address. For reasons of brevity, I will look at them specifically in relation to Paul – as the author of the majority of the epistles in the New Testament – although the issue applies to the other authors as well.

---

11. See the assessment in C. Clifton Black, 'Rhetorical Criticism', in Joel B. Green (ed.), *Hearing the New Testament: Strategies for Interpretation* (Grand Rapids: Eerdmans, 1995), pp. 256–277.
12. Brian K. Peterson, *Eloquence and the Proclamation of the Gospel in Corinth*, Society of Biblical Literature Dissertation Series (Atlanta: Scholars Press, 1998), pp. 31–32.

The first objection, raised by a number of scholars but most notably by Porter, is that we can't establish whether Paul was formally schooled in rhetoric, nor that he consciously used rhetoric in his letters.[13] This objection is adequately answered in studies by Stowers[14] and Judge[15] outlining the evidence that Paul received basic training in rhetoric, along with Classen's catalogue of the technical rhetorical terms that Paul uses throughout his letters.[16] Added to this is the undeniable observation that the Hellenistic world was a 'rhetorically saturated environment'[17] in which any educated person could not help but pick up the basics of rhetorical composition. As Watson points out, 'In Hellenistic culture rhetoric was central to secondary education and public oratory. Even if a New Testament writer *had not been formally educated*, rhetorical practice was everywhere and its forms would have been *familiar*' (italics mine).[18]

---

13. Stanley E. Porter, 'Rhetorical Categories in Pauline Literature', in Stanley E. Porter and Thomas H. Olbricht (eds.), *Rhetoric and the New Testament* (Sheffield: Sheffield Academic Press, 1993), p. 105. Jeffrey Weima ('What Does Aristotle Have to Do with Paul? An Evaluation of Rhetorical Criticism', *Calvin Theological Journal* 32 [1997], p. 465) agrees.

14. Stanley Kent Stowers, *A Rereading of Romans: Justice, Jews, and Gentiles* (New Haven: Yale University Press, 1994), p. 17.

15. Edwin Arthur Judge, 'Paul's Boasting in Relation to Contemporary Professional Practice', *Australian Biblical Review* 16 (1968), pp. 37–50.

16. Classen, *Rhetorical Criticism*, pp. 29–44.

17. Witherington, *NT Rhetoric*, p. 4.

18. Duane F. Watson, 'Rhetorical Criticism of Hebrews and the Catholic Epistles since 1978', *Currents in Research: Biblical Studies* 5 (1997), p. 177. See also George Alexander Kennedy, *New Testament Interpretation through Rhetorical Criticism*, Studies in Religion (Chapel Hill: University of North Carolina Press, 1984), p. 10; Richard N. Longenecker, *Galatians*, Word Biblical Commentary (Dallas: Word, 1990), p. cxiii; Carl J. Classen, 'St Paul's Epistles and Ancient Graeco-Roman Rhetoric', in Stanley E. Porter and Thomas H. Olbricht (eds.), *Rhetoric and the New Testament* (Sheffield: Sheffield Academic Press, 1993), p. 269.

Although some believe that Paul explicitly rejects using rhetoric (1 Cor. 1:17; 2:1, 4),[19] this was specifically a rejection of *sophistic* rhetoric (and the status claims associated with it) which emphasized style over substance. It was not a rejection of persuasive techniques or rhetorical forms *per se*.[20] In fact, Paul's disavowal of this kind of crowd-pleasing rhetoric in favour of 'plain speaking' is a well-attested rhetorical technique in itself![21]

The second objection, again raised by Porter (and others), is that the ancients themselves did not apply their theories of how to write *speeches* to the composition of *letters*.[22] However, this overlooks the oral nature of letters, particularly those written to a group of people (meaning they had to be read out loud). Indeed, there are many hints in Paul's letters that they were to be read out to an audience (e.g. 1 Thess. 5:27; Col. 4:16),[23] and that the epistolary opening and

---

19. Duane A. Litfin, *St Paul's Theology of Proclamation: 1 Corinthians 1–4 and Greco-Roman Rhetoric*, Society for New Testament Studies Monograph Series (Cambridge: Cambridge University Press, 1994), pp. 247–250.

20. Ben Witherington III, *Conflict and Community in Corinth: A Socio-Rhetorical Commentary on 1 and 2 Corinthians* (Grand Rapids: Eerdmans, 1995), pp. 46–47; Stephen M. Pogoloff, *Logos and Sophia: The Rhetorical Situation of 1 Corinthians*, Society of Biblical Literature Dissertation Series (Atlanta: Scholars Press, 1992), pp. 120–121; André Resner, *Preacher and Cross: Person and Message in Theology and Rhetoric* (Grand Rapids: Eerdmans, 1999), p. 4.

21. Classen, *Rhetorical Criticism*, p. 44. See also Judge, 'Paul's Boasting', p. 37; Pogoloff, *Logos and Sophia*, p. 136; Quintilian, *Institutes of Oratory*, 4.1.8–10.

22. Stanley E. Porter, 'The Theoretical Justification for Application of Rhetorical Categories to Pauline Epistolary Literature', in Stanley E. Porter and Thomas H. Olbricht (eds.), *Rhetoric and the New Testament* (Sheffield: Sheffield Academic Press, 1993), p. 109. See also Jeffrey T. Reed, 'Using Ancient Rhetorical Categories to Interpret Paul's Letters: A Question of Genre', ibid., p. 308.

23. On this, see Raymond F. Collins, '"I Command That This Letter Be Read": Writing as a Manner of Speaking', in Karl P. Donfried and Johannes Beutler (eds.), *The Thessalonian Debate: Methodological Discord or Methodological Synthesis?* (Grand Rapids: Eerdmans, 2000), pp. 319–339.

closing function merely as a kind of wrapping for a recorded speech[24] (and in Hebrews, the writer ends his letter with the usual letter greetings, but then in 13:22 refers to it as a 'word of exhortation' – the term for a homily). Letters were commonly seen as (somewhat inferior) substitutes for the writers' personal presence and the speech they would give if present.[25] Hughes also presents some compelling evidence from handbooks and theorists employing rhetorical theory and terminology in the context of letter-writing instruction.[26] Perhaps Quintilian sums it up best when he says that 'to speak well and to write well are but the same thing, and that a written oration is nothing but a record of an oration delivered'.[27]

In sum, the evidence strongly suggests that Paul would have received at least some rudimentary training in rhetoric and lived in a 'rhetoric-saturated environment', and that he wrote what were essentially oral texts, wrapped in the form of a letter, as a substitute for his personal presence. By this (and the other arguments presented in my previous book) I conclude that it *is* appropriate to analyse Paul's epistles – and, by similar arguments, the other New Testament epistles – using the conventions of Graeco-Roman rhetoric as described in the handbooks of the day.

---

24. There are many surviving examples of different genres being 'wrapped' in a letter; see David E. Aune, *The New Testament in Its Literary Environment*, 1st edn, Library of Early Christianity 8 (Philadelphia: Westminster Press, 1987), p. 170.

25. John L. White, *Light from Ancient Letters*, Foundations and Facets (Philadelphia: Fortress, 1986), p. 191; Aune, *NT in Its Literary Environment*, p. 197; J. Murphy-O'Connor, *Paul the Letter-Writer: His World, His Options, His Skills* (Collegeville: Liturgical Press, 1995), p. 65.

26. Frank Hughes, 'The Rhetoric of Letters', in Karl P. Donfried and Johannes Beutler (eds.), *The Thessalonian Debate: Methodological Discord or Methodological Synthesis?* (Grand Rapids: Eerdmans, 2000), pp. 194–240. See Pseudo-Demetrius, *On Elocution*, 223–235; Aristotle, *Rhetoric*, 3.12.2; Quintilian, *Institutes of Oratory*, 9.4.19.

27. Quintilian, *Institutes*, 12.10.51. Similarly, Cicero, *Letters to Atticus*, 8.4.

See also . . .

- Frank Hughes, 'The Rhetoric of Letters', in Karl P. Donfried and Johannes Beutler (eds.), *The Thessalonian Debate: Methodological Discord or Methodological Synthesis?* (Grand Rapids: Eerdmans, 2000), pp. 194–240.
- Tim MacBride, *Preaching the New Testament as Rhetoric: The Promise of Rhetorical Criticism for Expository Preaching* (Eugene: Wipf & Stock, 2014), pp. 22–34.
- Ben Witherington III, *New Testament Rhetoric: An Introductory Guide to the Art of Persuasion in and of the New Testament* (Eugene: Cascade, 2009), p. 242.

Read it for yourself

The source material for much of this is the ancient handbooks. They are readily available in English translation online, and are worth reading sometime in order to get the 'flavour' of how the ancients wrote about rhetoric. I've listed the key works below, with a URL that was current at the time of printing, and you can also find most at <https://openlibrary.org/read> or through a Web search.

- Aristotle, *The Art of Rhetoric*, <http://rhetoric.eserver.org/aristotle/>
- Quintilian, *Institutes of Oratory*, <http://rhetoric.eserver.org/quintilian/>
- Cicero, *On Oratory*, <https://archive.org/details/ciceroonoratoryaoociceuoft>

Two anonymous works:

- *Rhetoric to Alexander* (formerly ascribed to Aristotle), <https://archive.org/details/worksofaristotle11arisuoft>
- *Rhetoric to Herennius* (formerly ascribed to Cicero), <https://archive.org/stream/adcherenniumderaoocapluoft/>

APPENDIX B: THE RHETORICAL GENRE OF NEW TESTAMENT EPISTLES

Below is a *very brief* summary of the rhetorical genre of the relevant New Testament texts as I understand them.[1] When preaching a series on one of the epistles, early on in the process consult a variety of commentaries on this question of genre. I've recommended a few commentaries/essays which take into account a rhetorical approach.

Romans is one of the more debated letters, largely because of the uncertainty of the situation in Rome. Was Paul urging new behaviour in the light of the gospel (deliberative) or affirming what they already held (epideictic)? The presence of complex argumentation and diatribe points strongly in the direction of deliberative rhetoric.

---

1. Most of this is drawn from Ben Witherington III's commentaries, as well as from the survey of Paul's letters in Duane F. Watson, 'The Three Species of Rhetoric and the Study of the Pauline Epistles', in J. Paul Sampley and Peter Lampe (eds.), *Paul and Rhetoric* (New York: T & T Clark, 2010), pp. 25–47.

- Philip Esler, *Conflict and Identity in Romans* (Minneapolis: Fortress, 2003).
- Frank Matera, *Romans*, Paideia (Grand Rapids: Baker, 2010).
- Ben Witherington III, *Paul's Letter to the Romans* (Grand Rapids: Eerdmans, 2004).

1 Corinthians is deliberative, appealing for unity in place of factionalism. The topic of unity was a common theme of deliberative rhetoric, and there are many appeals to advantage and the 'common good'.

- Margaret Mitchell, *Paul and the Rhetoric of Reconciliation* (Louisville: Westminster John Knox Press, 1993).
- Pheme Perkins, *First Corinthians*, Paideia (Grand Rapids: Baker, 2012).
- Stephen M. Pogoloff, *Logos and Sophia: The Rhetorical Situation of 1 Corinthians* (Atlanta: Scholars Press, 1992).
- Ben Witherington III, *Conflict and Community in Corinth* (Grand Rapids: Eerdmans, 1995).

2 Corinthians is disputed, largely because of theories about whether the text we have contains more than one of Paul's letters merged together (as the alleged source letters may be of different genres).[2] Most would say that the overall species is deliberative, urging the Corinthians to reconcile with Paul, with forensic elements in support, defending Paul against accusations. A minority would see the reverse. As long as both elements are acknowledged, it makes little practical difference.

- Fredrick Long, *Ancient Rhetoric and Paul's Apology: The Compositional Unity of 2 Corinthians*, Society for New Testament Studies Monograph Series (Cambridge: CUP, 2004).

---

2. For an excellent argument against these partition theories, in the light of rhetorical theory, see Fredrick J. Long, *Ancient Rhetoric and Paul's Apology: The Compositional Unity of 2 Corinthians*, Society for New Testament Studies Monograph Series (Cambridge: Cambridge University Press, 2004).

- Ben Witherington III, *Conflict and Community in Corinth* (Grand Rapids: Eerdmans, 1995).

Galatians is seen as deliberative, persuading the hearers against adopting the Judaizers' recommended course of action. Early on it was thought of as forensic, since Paul gives a long defence of his apostleship in the first two chapters.[3] This is now seen as contributing to the overall deliberative aim.

- Mark Nanos, *The Galatians Debate: Contemporary Issues in Rhetorical and Historical Interpretation* (Peabody: Hendrickson, 2002).
- Ben Witherington III, *Grace in Galatia* (Grand Rapids: Eerdmans, 1998).

Ephesians is epideictic in praise of God (1:3), thereby urging a life lived in imitation of him (4:1).

- James Gregory, 'The Letter to the Ephesians: A Biblioblog Devoted to All Things Ephesians', <http://allthingsephesians.wordpress.com>
- Roy R. Jeal, 'Rhetorical Argumentation in Ephesians', in Anders Eriksson, Thomas H. Olbricht and Walter Übelacker (eds.), *Rhetorical Argumentation in Biblical Texts*, Emory Studies in Early Christianity 8 (Harrisburg: Trinity Press International, 2002), pp. 310–324.
- Andrew T. Lincoln, *Ephesians*, Word Biblical Commentary (Waco: Word, 1990).
- Ben Witherington III, *The Letters to Philemon, the Colossians, and the Ephesians* (Grand Rapids: Eerdmans, 2007).

Philippians is deliberative, urging them to prioritize their heavenly citizenship over their earthly one. There are some epideictic passages which seek to honour those who live by this advice (e.g. Jesus, Timothy and Epaphroditus).

---

3. Hans Dieter Betz, 'Literary Composition and Function of Paul's Letter to the Galatians', *New Testament Studies* 21 (1975), pp. 353–379.

- James W. Thompson and Bruce W. Longenecker, *Philippians and Philemon*, Paideia (Grand Rapids: Baker, 2016).
- Duane F. Watson, 'A Rhetorical Analysis of Philippians, and Its Implications for the Unity Question', *Novum Testamentum* 30 (1988), pp. 57–88.
- Ben Witherington III, *Paul's Letter to the Philippians: A Socio-Rhetorical Commentary* (Grand Rapids: Eerdmans, 2011).

Colossians is deliberative, and very similar to Galatians in its aim. It dissuades the audience from being 'taken captive' through the 'hollow and deceptive philosophy' which threatened to lead them away from Christ and back into slavery.

- Barth L. Campbell, 'Colossians 2:6–15 as a Thesis: A Rhetorical-Critical Study', *Journal for the Study of Rhetorical Criticism of the New Testament*, <http://rhetjournal.net/RhetJournal/Articles_files/Campbell.pdf>.
- Brian Walsh and Sylvia Keesmaat, *Colossians Remixed* (Downers Grove: InterVarsity Press, 2004).
- Ben Witherington III, *The Letters to Philemon, the Colossians, and the Ephesians* (Grand Rapids: Eerdmans, 2007).

1 Thessalonians is epideictic, celebrating the hearers' recently established faith and encouraging them to keep going in it all the more.

- Frank Hughes, 'The Rhetoric of 1 Thessalonians', in Raymond F. Collins and Norbert Baumert (eds.), *The Thessalonian Correspondence* (Louvain: Leuven University Press, 1990).
- Ben Witherington III, *1 & 2 Thessalonians* (Grand Rapids: Eerdmans, 2006).

2 Thessalonians is deliberative, urging right behaviour so as to be found worthy when Christ returns.

- Ben Witherington III, *1 & 2 Thessalonians* (Grand Rapids: Eerdmans, 2006).

Philemon is deliberative, and follows the (deliberative) genre of a letter of reconciliation. Paul is seeking to persuade Philemon to be reconciled with Onesimus, his former slave.

- James W. Thompson and Bruce W. Longenecker, *Philippians and Philemon*, Paideia (Grand Rapids: Baker, 2016).
- Ben Witherington III, *The Letters to Philemon, the Colossians, and the Ephesians* (Grand Rapids: Eerdmans, 2007).

Hebrews is self-consciously a sermon (13:22) which uses the deliberative strategy of presenting two courses of action and two destinies. The audience are encouraged not to 'shrink back' or 'fall away', which leads to destruction, but to 'have faith' and 'persevere', which leads to salvation and reward. There are, however, numerous epideictic sections which honour those who have persevered and shame those who have fallen away.

- David A. deSilva, *Perseverance in Gratitude* (Grand Rapids: Eerdmans, 2000).
- James W. Thompson, *Hebrews* (Grand Rapids: Baker, 2008).
- Ben Witherington III, *Letters and Homilies for Jewish Christians: A Socio-Rhetorical Commentary on Hebrews, James and Jude* (Downers Grove: InterVarsity Press, 2007).

1 Peter is deliberative, calling for holiness in a hostile world, and reminding the audience that it's God's judgment that ultimately counts, not that of the world.

- Duane Watson and Terrance Callan, *First and Second Peter*, Paideia (Grand Rapids: Baker, 2012).
- Ben Witherington III, *Letters and Homilies for Hellenized Christians: A Socio-Rhetorical Commentary on 1–2 Peter*, vol. 2 (Downers Grove: InterVarsity Press, 2007).

2 Peter is probably epideictic, encouraging those already 'established' in the truth (1:12) to continue to live in this way and so 'confirm' their calling (1:10).

- Joel B. Green, *1 Peter* (Grand Rapids: Eerdmans, 2007).

- Duane Watson and Terrance Callan, *First and Second Peter*, Paideia (Grand Rapids: Baker, 2012).
- Ben Witherington III, *Letters and Homilies for Hellenized Christians: A Socio-Rhetorical Commentary on 1–2 Peter*, vol. 2 (Downers Grove: InterVarsity Press, 2007).

1 John is epideictic, reinforcing community values and group identity in the wake of the departure of some from among their number.[4]

- George Parsenios, *First, Second, and Third John*, Paideia (Grand Rapids: Baker, 2014).
- Duane Watson, 'Amplification Techniques in 1 John: The Interaction of Rhetorical Style and Invention', *Journal for the Study of the New Testament* 51 (1993), pp. 99–123.
- Ben Witherington III, *Letters and Homilies for Hellenized Christians: A Socio-Rhetorical Commentary on Titus, 1–2 Timothy and 1–3 John*, vol. 1 (Downers Grove: InterVarsity Press, 2006).

---

4. See Tim MacBride, 'Aliens and Strangers: Minority Group Rhetoric in the Later New Testament Writings', in M. Harding and A. Nobbs (eds.), *Into All the World* (Grand Rapids: Eerdmans, 2016).

BIBLIOGRAPHY

Anthony, Michael J., and James Riley Estep (eds.), *Management Essentials for Christian Ministries* (Nashville: B&H, 2005).

Aune, David E., *The New Testament in Its Literary Environment*, 1st edn, Library of Early Christianity 8 (Philadelphia: Westminster, 1987).

—— 'The Use and Abuse of the Enthymeme in New Testament Scholarship', *New Testament Studies* 48 (2003), pp. 299–320.

Berger, Peter L., *A Rumor of Angels: Modern Society and the Rediscovery of the Supernatural*, 1st edn (Garden City, NY: Doubleday, 1969).

Betz, Hans Dieter, 'Literary Composition and Function of Paul's Letter to the Galatians', *New Testament Studies* 21 (1975), pp. 353–379.

Black, C. Clifton, 'Rhetorical Criticism', in Joel B. Green (ed.), *Hearing the New Testament: Strategies for Interpretation* (Grand Rapids: Eerdmans, 1995), pp. 256–277.

Bruce, F. F., *1 and 2 Thessalonians*, Word Biblical Commentary (Dallas: Word, 1982).

Buttrick, David, *Homiletic: Moves and Structures* (Philadelphia: Fortress, 1987).

—— 'Interpretation and Preaching', *Interpretation* 25 (1981), pp. 43–58.

Campbell, Barth L., 'Colossians 2:6–15 as a Thesis: A Rhetorical-Critical Study', *Journal for the Study of Rhetorical Criticism of the New Testament*, <http://rhetjournal.net/RhetJournal/Articles_files/Campbell.pdf>, accessed 22 January 2016.

Cialdini, Robert B., *Influence: The Psychology of Persuasion*, rev. edn (New York: HarperCollins, 2007).

Classen, Carl J., *Rhetorical Criticism of the New Testament* (Boston: Brill, 2002).

—— 'St Paul's Epistles and Ancient Graeco-Roman Rhetoric', in Stanley E. Porter and Thomas H. Olbricht (eds.), *Rhetoric and the New Testament* (Sheffield: Sheffield Academic Press, 1993), pp. 265–291.

Cloud, Henry, *9 Things You Simply Must Do to Succeed in Love and Life* (Nashville: Integrity, 2004).

Collins, Raymond F., '"I Command That This Letter Be Read": Writing as a Manner of Speaking', in Karl P. Donfried and Johannes Beutler (eds.), *The Thessalonian Debate: Methodological Discord or Methodological Synthesis?* (Grand Rapids: Eerdmans, 2000), pp. 319–339.

Craddock, Fred B., *Preaching* (Nashville: Abingdon Press, 1985).

Danker, Frederick W., *Benefactor: Epigraphic Study of a Graeco-Roman and New Testament Semantic Field* (St Louis: Clayton, 1982).

Debanné, Marc J., *Enthymemes in the Letters of Paul*, T & T Clark Library of Biblical Studies (London: T & T Clark, 2006).

de Brauw, Michael, 'The Parts of the Speech', in Ian Worthington (ed.), *A Companion to Greek Rhetoric* (Malden, MA: Blackwell, 2007), pp. 187–202.

deSilva, David A., *An Introduction to the New Testament: Contexts, Methods and Ministry Formation* (Downers Grove: InterVarsity Press, 2004).

—— *Perseverance in Gratitude: A Socio-Rhetorical Commentary on the Epistle 'to the Hebrews'* (Grand Rapids: Eerdmans, 2000).

Dever, Mark, *The Message of the New Testament: Promises Kept* (Wheaton: Crossway, 2005).

Eriksson, Anders, 'Fear of Eternal Damnation: *Pathos* Appeal in 1 Corinthians 15 and 16', in Thomas H. Olbricht and Jerry L. Sumney (eds.), *Paul and Pathos* (Atlanta: SBL, 2001), pp. 115–126.

Fee, Gordon, *Philippians*, New International Commentary on the New Testament (Grand Rapids: Eerdmans, 1995).

Giglio, Louie, *How Great Is Our God*, Passion Talk Series (2009; DVD; Six Step Records, 2012).

Hogan, Lucy Lind, 'Rethinking Persuasion: Developing an Incarnational Theology of Preaching', *Homiletic* 24, no. 2 (1999), pp. 1–12.

—— and Robert Reid, *Connecting with the Congregation: Rhetoric and the Art of Preaching* (Nashville: Abingdon Press, 1999).

Holloway, Paul A., 'The Enthymeme as an Element of Style in Paul', *Journal of Biblical Literature* 120, no. 2 (2001): pp. 329–343.

Hughes, Frank, 'The Rhetoric of 1 Thessalonians', in Raymond F. Collins and Norbert Baumert (eds.), *The Thessalonian Correspondence* (Louvain: Leuven University Press, 1990), pp. 94–116.

—— 'The Rhetoric of Letters', in Karl P. Donfried and Johannes Beutler (eds.), *The Thessalonian Debate: Methodological Discord or Methodological Synthesis?* (Grand Rapids: Eerdmans, 2000), pp. 194–240.

Huttar, David K., *Galatians: The Gospel According to Paul*, The Deeper Life Pulpit Commentary (Camp Hill: Christian Publications, 2001).

Hybels, Bill, *Courageous Leadership* (Grand Rapids: Zondervan, 2002).

Judge, Edwin Arthur, 'Paul's Boasting in Relation to Contemporary Professional Practice', *Australian Biblical Review* 16 (1968), pp. 37–50.

Keck, Leander E., '*Pathos* in Romans? Mostly Preliminary Remarks', in Thomas H. Olbricht and Jerry L. Sumney (eds.), *Paul and Pathos* (Atlanta: SBL, 2001), pp. 71–96.

Kennedy, George Alexander, *New Testament Interpretation through Rhetorical Criticism*, Studies in Religion (Chapel Hill: University of North Carolina Press, 1984).

Kraftchik, Steven J., 'Πάθη in Paul: The Emotional Logic of "Original Argument"', in Thomas H. Olbricht and Jerry L. Sumney (eds.), *Paul and Pathos* (Atlanta: SBL, 2001), pp. 39–70.

Kurz, William S., 'Narrative Models for Imitation in Luke–Acts', in Abraham J. Malherbe, David L. Balch, Everett Ferguson and Wayne A. Meeks (eds.), *Greeks, Romans, and Christians: Essays in Honor of Abraham J. Malherbe* (Minneapolis: Fortress, 1990), pp. 171–189.

Litfin, Duane A., *St Paul's Theology of Proclamation: 1 Corinthians 1–4 and Greco-Roman Rhetoric*, Society for New Testament Studies Monograph Series (Cambridge: Cambridge University Press, 1994).

Long, Fredrick J., *Ancient Rhetoric and Paul's Apology: The Compositional Unity of 2 Corinthians*, Society for New Testament Studies Monograph Series (Cambridge: Cambridge University Press, 2004).

Long, Thomas G., *The Witness of Preaching*, 1st edn (Louisville: Westminster John Knox Press, 1989).

Longenecker, Richard N., *Galatians*, Word Biblical Commentary (Dallas: Word, 1990).

Low, Alvin, *Descending Into Greatness: Biblical Leadership* (Morrisville, NC: Lulu, 2006).

MacBride, Tim, 'Aliens and Strangers: Minority Group Rhetoric in the Later New Testament Writings', in M. Harding and A. Nobbs (eds.), *Into All the World* (Grand Rapids: Eerdmans, 2016).

—— *Preaching the New Testament as Rhetoric: The Promise of Rhetorical Criticism for Expository Preaching*, Australian College of Theology Monograph Series (Eugene: Wipf & Stock, 2014).

McKnight, Scot, *Galatians: From Biblical Text . . . to Contemporary Life*, NIV Application Commentary (Grand Rapids: Zondervan, 1995).

Mathewson, Dana, *Call 2 Ministry: Exploring the Myths, the Mystery, and the Meaning of Following God's Call into Vocational Ministry* (Maitland, FL: Xulon, 2003).

Mitchell, Margaret M., *Paul and the Rhetoric of Reconciliation* (Louisville: Westminster John Knox Press, 1993).

Momigliano, Arnaldo, *On Pagans, Jews, and Christians*, 1st edn (Middletown, CT: Wesleyan University Press, 1987).

Morrison, Michael, *Enthymemes in Hebrews*, Kindle Edition (Amazon Digital Services, 2010).

Muilenburg, James, 'Form Criticism and Beyond', *Journal of Biblical Literature* 88 (1969), pp. 1–18.

Murphy, J., *Rhetoric in the Middle Ages: A History of Rhetorical Theory from St Augustine to the Renaissance* (Berkeley: University of California Press, 1974).

Murphy-O'Connor, J., *Paul the Letter-Writer: His World, His Options, His Skills* (Collegeville: Liturgical Press, 1995).

Neyrey, Jerome H., *Honor and Shame in the Gospel of Matthew*, 1st edn (Louisville: Westminster John Knox Press, 1998).

Olbricht, Thomas H., '*Pathos* as Proof in Greco-Roman Rhetoric', in Thomas H. Olbricht and Jerry L. Sumney (eds.), *Paul and Pathos* (Atlanta: SBL, 2001), pp. 7–22.

Peterson, Brian K., *Eloquence and the Proclamation of the Gospel in Corinth*, Society of Biblical Literature Dissertation Series (Atlanta: Scholars Press, 1998).

Peterson, Eugene H., *Traveling Light: Modern Meditations on St Paul's Letter of Freedom* (Colorado Springs: Helmers & Howard, 1988).

Pogoloff, Stephen M., *Logos and Sophia: The Rhetorical Situation of 1 Corinthians*, Society of Biblical Literature Dissertation Series (Atlanta: Scholars Press, 1992).

Porter, Stanley E., 'Rhetorical Categories in Pauline Literature', in Stanley E. Porter and Thomas H. Olbricht (eds.), *Rhetoric and the New Testament* (Sheffield: Sheffield Academic Press, 1993), pp. 100–122.

—— 'The Theoretical Justification for Application of Rhetorical Categories to Pauline Epistolary Literature', in Stanley E. Porter and Thomas H. Olbricht (eds.), *Rhetoric and the New Testament* (Sheffield: Sheffield Academic Press, 1993), pp. 100–122.

—— and Thomas H. Olbricht (eds.), *Rhetoric and the New Testament: Essays from the 1992 Heidelberg Conference*, Journal for the Study of the New Testament Supplement Series, vol. 90 (Sheffield: Sheffield Academic Press, 1993).

Quicke, Michael J., *360-Degree Preaching: Hearing, Speaking, and Living the Word* (Grand Rapids: Baker Academic, 2003).

Reed, Jeffrey T., 'Using Ancient Rhetorical Categories to Interpret Paul's Letters: A Question of Genre', in Stanley E. Porter and Thomas H. Olbricht (eds.), *Rhetoric and the New Testament* (Sheffield: Sheffield Academic Press, 1993), pp. 292–324.

Resner, André, *Preacher and Cross: Person and Message in Theology and Rhetoric* (Grand Rapids: Eerdmans, 1999).

Robinson, Haddon W., *Biblical Preaching: The Development and Delivery of Expository Messages*, 2nd edn (Grand Rapids: Baker Academic, 2001).

Rose, Lucy Atkinson, *Sharing the Word: Preaching in the Roundtable Church*, 1st edn (Louisville: Westminster John Knox Press, 1997).

Stamps, Dennis L., 'Rhetorical Criticism of the New Testament: Ancient and Modern Evaluations of Argumentation', in Stanley E. Porter and David Tombs (eds.), *Approaches to New Testament Study*, Journal for the Study of the New Testament Supplement Series (Sheffield: Sheffield Academic Press, 1995).

Stowers, Stanley Kent, *A Rereading of Romans: Justice, Jews, and Gentiles* (New Haven: Yale University Press, 1994).

Swift, Robert C., 'The Theme and Structure of Philippians', *Bibliotheca Sacra* 141, no. 563 (1984), pp. 234–254.

Thielman, Frank, *Philippians*, NIV Application Commentary (Grand Rapids: Zondervan, 1995).

Thompson, James W., *Preaching Like Paul: Homiletical Wisdom for Today*, 1st edn (Louisville: Westminster John Knox Press, 2001).

Watson, Duane F., 'Rhetorical Criticism of Hebrews and the Catholic Epistles since 1978', *Currents in Research: Biblical Studies* 5 (1997), pp. 175–207.

—— 'The Three Species of Rhetoric and the Study of the Pauline Epistles', in J. Paul Sampley and Peter Lampe (eds.), *Paul and Rhetoric* (New York: T & T Clark, 2010), pp. 25–47.

—— and Alan J. Hauser, *Rhetorical Criticism of the Bible: A Comprehensive Bibliography with Notes on History and Method*, Biblical Interpretation Series (Leiden: Brill, 1994).

Weima, Jeffrey, 'What Does Aristotle Have to Do with Paul? An Evaluation of Rhetorical Criticism', *Calvin Theological Journal* 32 (1997), pp. 458–468.

Welborn, Larry L., *Politics and Rhetoric in the Corinthian Epistles* (Macon, GA: Mercer University Press, 1997).

White, John L., *Light from Ancient Letters*, Foundations and Facets (Philadelphia: Fortress, 1986).

Witherington III, Ben, *Conflict and Community in Corinth: A Socio-Rhetorical Commentary on 1 and 2 Corinthians* (Grand Rapids: Eerdmans, 1995).

—— *Grace in Galatia: A Commentary on St Paul's Letter to the Galatians* (Grand Rapids: Eerdmans, 1998).

—— *New Testament Rhetoric: An Introductory Guide to the Art of Persuasion in and of the New Testament* (Eugene: Cascade, 2009).

—— *Paul's Letter to the Philippians: A Socio-Rhetorical Commentary* (Grand Rapids: Eerdmans, 2011).

—— and Darlene Hyatt, *Paul's Letter to the Romans: A Socio-Rhetorical Commentary* (Grand Rapids: Eerdmans, 2004).

Wuellner, William, 'Where Is Rhetorical Criticism Taking Us?', *Catholic Biblical Quarterly* 49 (1987), pp. 448–463.

Yancey, Philip, *Where Is God When It Hurts?*, rev. edn (Grand Rapids: Zondervan, 1990).

INDEX OF SCRIPTURE REFERENCES